Night-vision goggles

Handheld transmitter

Laptop computer trace showing presence of bug in a building

James Bond's piton gun from *Goldeneye*

Side view of explosives pack for stay-behind agents in the event of World War III occurring

Ultraviolet lantern and anti-bugging seals

Prints made by SOE agent's rubber soles used to disguise beach landings

Ox tongue tin for
smuggling maps and
compasses, World War I

# EYEWITNESS BOOKS

# SPY

German invisible ink
and sponge

Written by
## Richard Platt
Photographed by
## Geoff Dann and Steve Gorton

SOE rubber soles
worn on boots to
disguise landings on
beaches and in deserts

Leather boot heel
with concealed
compartment,
World
War II

Message hidden
in rubber boot
heel, World
War II

ALFRED A. KNOPF • NEW YORK

Counter-
espionage
mirror for
looking
around
corners

Transmitter
for bugging
room

## A DORLING KINDERSLEY BOOK

**Project editor**  Miranda Smith
**Art editor**  Kati Poynor
**Assistant editor**  Julie Ferris
**Managing editor**  Gillian Denton
**Managing art editor**  Julia Harris
**Production**  Charlotte Trail
**Picture research**  Sarah Moule

Printed in Singapore
0 9 8 7 6 5 4 3 2

**Library of Congress Cataloging-in-Publication Data**
Platt, Richard.
Spy / written by Richard Platt.
p.  cm. — (Eyewitness Books)
Includes index.
Summary: Presents information about men and women spies
throughout history as well as about the tools and equipment they
used in espionage and intelligence service.
1. Espionage—History—Juvenile literature. 2. Intelligence
service—History—Juvenile literature. [1. Espionage—
History. 2. Intelligence service—History.] I. Title.
II.Series
JF1525.16P583   1996
327.12—dc20   96-11003
ISBN 0-679-88122-0 (trade)
ISBN 0-679-98122-5 (lib. bdg.)

Color reproduction by
Colourscan, Singapore
Printed in Singapore by Toppan

Silk map of
France used
by wartime
agent

Handheld
transmitter
or "bug"

Doll made in Fresnes
prison, France, by World
War II agent Odette Sansom

Matchbox created for Special
Operations Executive agent

# Contents

Capsule for suicide pill, World War II

Suicide pill, World War II

Handheld receiver and earpiece

# What is a spy?

SPYING, WHICH IS ALSO called espionage, began thousands of years ago, with nations battling for land, wealth, or slaves. Spies sneaked into the camps of their enemies, counting the number of warriors or looking for plans of attack. If they were successful, they returned as heroes with the "intelligence," secrets, they had uncovered. Those who were caught faced execution. Throughout history governments and businesses have hidden their most important documents, very often marking them with special phrases such as "TOP SECRET" or "CONFIDENTIAL," and allowing only a few trusted people to see them. Spies are hired by other nations or businesses to find out this secret information. Spies still live dangerous lives today. Some work like burglars to collect intelligence. Others have access to secrets only because other people trust them. By betraying that trust, a spy can win or lose wars, and even change the course of history.

*Rahab marked her windows with a red cord*

*Joshua watches as the walls of Jericho tumble down*

*Tapestry shows spies from both sides in the Battle of Hastings*

**BIBLE ESPIONAGE**
A story in the Old Testament, the holy book of Judaism and Christianity, tells how spies helped defeat the walled city of Jericho. The leader of the attacking army, Joshua, sent two spies into the town at dusk. They went to the house of a prostitute, Rahab, and hid on the roof. Rahab lied to the Jericho authorities to protect the spies, and when Joshua's troops destroyed the city, they spared the lives of Rahab and her family, but killed everybody else.

**EGYPTIAN SPY**
Ankhesenamen, young queen of Egypt, wanted to remarry when her husband, Tutankhamen, died in 1324 B.C. She wrote to a neighboring king: "Send me one of your grown-up sons ... he shall be king over Egypt." Instead, the king sent his assistant as a spy to check the queen's story.

## ALEXANDER THE GREAT
The Macedonian king Alexander the Great (356–323 B.C.) used spies to find out about enemies' troop movements, and also to scout the best marching routes for his massive armies. Alexander's spies used a simple but effective technique to keep their messages secret. They wrote on narrow scrolls spiraling around a stick. Unwinding the scroll broke up the words of the message. But when wound around an identical stick, the text was easy to read.

## SPYING FOR THE MONGOLS
Spies helped Genghis Khan (1162–1227) to conquer most of Asia. Genghis came from Mongolia in central Asia, but he knew that people from Mongolia would soon arouse suspicion in distant lands. So Khan shrewdly recruited spies from among the target peoples, and these local spies were able to move around freely, collecting intelligence. Over longer distances, he used horsemen who could ride ten times faster than a marching army to carry his secret messages.

*In the east, the Mongol empire reached the Pacific*

*The Bayeux Tapestry is actually embroidery on a linen strip 230 ft (70 m) long*

## UNNOTICED IN THE CROWD
Some of the greatest spies of the past have been female: women could often go unnoticed where a man would arouse suspicion. In wartime, almost all young men joined the armed forces, and a man in civilian clothes was an unusual sight. In this photograph of Dutch spies at work during World War II (1939–45), one of the women takes a picture with a hidden camera.

*Patterned bag hides camera lens*

*Fictional spy "007" was given a special "license to kill"*

## RECORDED FOR POSTERITY
The Bayeux Tapestry shows spies in the historic Battle of Hastings in England in 1066. The tapestry records how an army from northwest France, led by William of Normandy (1028–1087), conquered England in 1066. English spies reported sighting thousands of clean-shaven men with short hair. At that time in England, all men except priests wore mustaches and long hair, so the spies assumed that they had seen thousands of French priests. In fact, these "priests" were soldiers, who greatly outnumbered the English.

## FICTIONAL SPIES
Glamorous spy James Bond, agent 007, is the hero of 13 novels by English author Ian Lancaster Fleming (1908–64). Fleming was himself a spy before he began his career as a writer. He used the people he met during that time as models for the characters in his books. The plots of the books and the Bond films leave out the routine side of the lives of real spies. However, some of Fleming's own exploits were as daring as those of the fictional agent 007.

# Types of spy

Spies come from many different backgrounds and are recruited by an espionage agency for a variety of reasons. Many spies are attracted by money, but some are motivated by deeply held beliefs and are called "walk-in" spies because they require no persuasion. Others spy because they are being blackmailed, and still more because it makes them feel important. As "plants," spies penetrate (work their way into) a target organization, where they can collect intelligence. However, recruiting an "agent in place" is sometimes easier than penetration. These trusted insiders have access to secrets even before an agency recruits them – perhaps by using bribery or blackmail.

**TROUBADOURS**
These medieval minstrels went from castle to castle entertaining European nobles. Some spied by listening to royal gossip and repeating the news when they traveled to another country.

**CARELESS TALK**
Spies do not make themselves obvious by wearing uniforms! This wartime poster warned British citizens that they should not gossip about sons and husbands in the armed forces because "Careless talk costs lives." Bus passengers listening to the conversation might be spies and could report details of troop movements to the enemy.

*Walker tramped Vienna's streets while Soviet agents checked that he was not being followed*

*Building (indicated by red arrow on map) mentioned in Walker's typed instructions for a 1978 visit to Vienna*

**INSIDER TRAPPED**
French ambassador to Moscow Maurice Dejean unknowingly hired spies to work as his driver and maid. They used blackmail to try and turn him into an "agent in place." The plot failed, but Dejean's career was ruined.

**WALK-IN WALKER**
American John Walker worked for the U.S. Navy and sold intelligence to the Soviet Union for 17 years. To meet them for payment and training, his Soviet handlers usually instructed Walker to travel to Vienna, Austria.

*The splendidly dressed Russian diplomats are "boyars" – members of noble Russian families*

**AMATEUR SPIES**
Since Biblical times, traders have kept their eyes and ears open wide when they traveled abroad. These "amateur spies" are returning home from the land of Canaan to report what they have seen.

Iraq designed the "Supergun" to shell targets thousands of miles away

**EXPENDABLE SPIES**
MI6 (the British secret intelligence service) encouraged businesses to sell parts for weapons such as this "Supergun" to Iraq in the 1980s. The exporters brought back intelligence that was highly valued by MI6. However, the exporters were actually breaking an arms ban. The British government tried, and failed, to avoid embarrassment by denying the authorization of the sales.

**MOLE IN THE CIA**
Enemy agents who penetrate the security services sometimes earn the nickname of "mole," because they dig deep and work invisibly. Chinese-American mole Larry Wu Tai Chin worked for the CIA for more than 35 years. From the beginning he was a mole and was spying for China.

**SPIES AT COURT**
Most spies are "illegals" – if they are caught, they face prosecution and punishment. Throughout history, traders and merchants, such as the ones in this 16th-century woodcut, have been used as "illegals." Diplomats, on the other hand, are often called "legals." These civil servants represent their country in its embassies abroad, and they have a license to spy. If they are caught, their diplomatic status protects them from punishment under international law. In fact, very few actually work as spies. More are intelligence officers – they use their diplomatic jobs as a cover for recruiting and controlling spies.

Procession of diplomats and merchants at the court of the Austrian archduke Maximilian II

# Secret tool kit

THE CENTRAL INTELLIGENCE AGENCY (CIA) nickname "sneakies" neatly describes the tools, gadgets, and weapons on which undercover agents often rely. With the aid of a sneaky, a spy can "bug" a conversation or photograph a meeting. Other devices make escape easier or hide the evidence of espionage from prying eyes. Fictional spy James Bond made sneakies famous. Before a dangerous mission, he visited the workshop of "Q," who built such gadgets. Author Ian Fleming based Q's character on the inventor Charles Fraser Smith (1904–92), who designed the equipment for the British intelligence services in World War II. Other organizations had equally ingenious spy workshops – for example, Stanley Lovell (1890–1976) equipped spies in the United States.

A spoof spy kit for the wartime spy

*Pushing the two halves of the camera together advances the film by one frame and covers the lens*

*Lens is focused here*

**SUPER SMALL SNAPPER**
The Minox camera is small enough to hide in a fist, but takes photographs of excellent quality. The Latvian manufacturers originally sold the Minox as a pocket-size camera, but the intelligence services quickly realized its potential and it became standard spy equipment. The camera's only real problem was the tiny size of its negatives, which needed to be enlarged 25 times to be read. At this small scale a speck of dust on the film could obscure a vital word.

*Pen writes normally*

**HANDY HEEL**
Concealed items must be well hidden to escape discovery, and shoes and boots can hide quite large weapons or tools. In World War II, spies sometimes concealed gold, for bribery, and knives in their insoles.

*Thread is pulled to withdraw concealed item*

*Exposures took minutes, so fixed objects such as buildings were the only practical subjects*

*Acoustic tube to microphone*

*Camera took four pictures when agent uncovered the pinholes*

## PINHOLE CAMERA
Some of the tiniest spy cameras use pinholes instead of a lens. KGB agents used this one in the 1980s. The camera takes pictures that are not blurred however close or far away the object. Although, nothing is really sharp either!

## LISTENING PEN
The circuits of radio transmitters are now so small that spies can install bugs (small microphones) in the tiniest of objects. This pen is inconspicuous in a pocket, and would not attract attention in a desk drawer. However, it conceals a bug to eavesdrop on any nearby conversation. A tiny transmitter broadcasts the signal on UHF radio frequencies. The power of the signal is low, but strong enough for an accomplice sitting in a car almost 1,640 ft (500 m) away to pick up the conversation with a receiver and record it.

## A BRUSH WITH THE ENEMY
All spies risk capture, but the danger is perhaps even greater in wartime. So World War II spies hid all kinds of escape equipment in objects like this hairbrush. A compartment contains a saw to cut through prison bars, a map of enemy-occupied territory, and a compass.

*Body of pen conceals transmitter*

*Pulling bristles lifts compartment lid*

*Tube houses battery with enough power for up to six hours*

*Miniature saw blade*

*Compass*

*Compass needle*

*Devices hidden in hairbrush*

*Map printed on thin paper to fold up small*

*Base of brush is hollow*

## EASY ACCESS
The safest way to enter a locked building is to bribe a low-paid employee to unlock the door. When this is not possible, spies may try to pick the lock with specially shaped tools like these. In Britain, intelligence services employed a retired burglar to teach this vital skill to wartime agents.

*By inserting one of the hooked blades into a lock and turning gently, the tool lifts levers that hold the bolt in place*

*Specially shaped instruments are called picklocks*

*Range of picklocks enables agent to tackle locks of different sizes*

*Picks fold away into penknife-like handle*

## CHEATING AT CARDS
World War II spies concealed an escape map in a pack of playing cards. Tearing each card apart revealed a small area of the map. The numbers on each section allowed the spy to piece the whole map together like a jigsaw.

# Seeing the invisible

Visual surveillance is part of the training of all agents. They learn to use their eyes and their cameras to collect intelligence or to gather information to blackmail their enemies. They use technology to make their vision keener. Magnifying lenses give a closer view of private scenes, while some night-vision equipment makes photography possible even in a candlelit bedroom. However, the clearest pictures do not guarantee the success of a surveillance mission. When spies secretly photographed a Western diplomat with his girlfriend, they were sure they could use the pictures for blackmail. They met the diplomat and threatened to send the pictures to his wife. His shameless response shocked them. "What wonderful shots!" he exclaimed. "Can you make me copies?"

**CAUGHT IN THE ACT**
To photograph subjects in near darkness, spies can use image-intensifier cameras. These use a tube similar to those fitted to night-vision equipment (opposite). The camera makes photography possible in extremely dim conditions; the glow of a cigarette provides ample light to photograph an agent copying documents or passing secrets to an accomplice. Image intensifiers cannot record color, so spies usually load their cameras with sensitive black-and-white film. In color (left), pictures have an eerie green glow.

Agent using a night-vision pen

*A spy can swap a standard lens for a powerful telephoto*

*Replacing camera with an eyepiece turns the tube into a night vision telescope*

*Ordinary flashlight batteries in base provide power*

*Lens enlarges details six times more than a standard lens*

*Lugs for carrying strap*

*"Trigger" operates shutter*

An ordinary lens takes in the whole of the street market.

"Photo-sniper" camera picks out two particular figures from the crowd.

*The rifle grip helps steady camera and keeps photographs sharp when it is impractical to use a tripod*

Head harness is
adjustable for comfort

Two small batteries
power goggles
for hours

OH 1×20

Tubes make light
50,000 times
brighter

Twin lenses
allow spy to
judge distance

Eyepieces adjust
to suit the eyesight
of individual spies

Lenses form life-size
images so scene is
not distorted and
goggles can be used
for night-driving

**SEEING IN THE DARK**
Night vision goggles give
spies the ability to see in very
dim light. In total darkness an
infrared flashlight casts a bright
light upon the scene for anyone
wearing the goggles, but nothing
can be seen by the target. Most
of these systems work much
like the image-forming tubes
used on television cameras.
The tube converts photons (light
particles) from the camera lens
into electrons (tiny, electrically
charged particles). The electrons
speed towards a phosphor screen,
making a brilliant glow where
they strike it. The screen forms a
brighter copy of the original scene.

Strong harness
supports heavy
goggles

Side view of
night goggles

Rifle stock rests
against shoulder

**HAWK EYE**
Much surveillance work
relies on ordinary cameras
and lenses that any wealthy
photographer could buy over the
counter. However, this powerful
300 mm telephoto lens was specially
crafted for use by Soviet border guards
and intelligence agents. With it, Soviet
spies could close in on a distant scene
and photograph agents at work.

**ALL DONE WITH MIRRORS**
Spies in 19th-century France used these
innocent-looking binoculars to keep a
watch on their opponents. One lens
produced the same view as an ordinary
pair of binoculars. The other was a
dummy. Behind it, an angled mirror
gave a perfect view of whatever was
happening to one side – while the spy
appeared to be staring straight ahead.
A similar device is still available today.
Disguised as a lens hood, it enables spies
to photograph subjects at their side,
while pointing the camera forwards.

Real lens

Focusing
wheel

Dummy
lens

Real lens in side

Hole for angled mirror

15

# Bugs and taps

BEFORE YOU WHISPER "Tell me!" in a friend's ear, take a careful look around. Whispered words seem secret, but with bugs and wiretaps, spies can make sure that no conversation is really private. Bugs are hidden microphones, usually linked to radio transmitters, and like the insects they are named after, some are tiny. A spy who tunes a radio receiver to the correct frequency can hear every sound that reaches the bug, even if he or she is elsewhere. Telephone bugs or transmitters perform the same service each time a telephone is used. Tape recorders make it easy to monitor (check) wiretaps and bugs. When there is a sound, recording starts automatically; the tape stops after there have been a few moments of quiet.

**SENDING...**
A basic bug or transmitter can be very small indeed. This one is the size of a matchbox.

**...AND RECEIVING**
This pocket-sized receiver picks up signals from the bug (left), relaying them to headphones or a tape recorder. The bug is a "quick plant" type, small enough to hide behind a picture. Its battery lasts a week or so. The bug is cheap enough to abandon – returning to collect it doubles the risk of discovery.

The 8-in (20-cm) bug found inside seal

**EMBASSY SEAL**
A gift from the Soviet Union, this replica eagle seal of the United States decorated the U.S. embassy in Moscow. In fact, the seal housed an ingenious bug. Sound made a spring inside the seal vibrate. Spies in a nearby building were able to detect the vibrations and interpret the words that caused them by using radar.

CIA microphone wristwatch

**WHAT IS THE TIME?**
This CIA wristwatch conceals a microphone. It is normally inconspicuous, but in 1977, an American spy in Moscow betrayed himself because he had forgotten to remove his normal watch.

*Link to tape recorder hidden in agent's clothing*

**PHONE-TAPPING**
Telephone taps can be easier to place than bugs because spies need not enter the room they want to listen to. Unless there is a switchboard, a telephone tap can go anywhere between the telephone and the exchange. In this film reconstruction from *Stakeout*, Chris Lecce (played by Richard Dreyfuss) uses a wiretap to keep a vital witness in an organized crime case under surveillance.

**TELEPHONE BUG**
In a large building with a switchboard and many extensions, a spy would need to install taps on every line and then sift through many hours of tapes to hear just one short call. However, if a spy can enter the building unnoticed, a more practical solution is possible – fitting a bug to a particular telephone like the one on this page. The spy can then either eavesdrop directly or record all conversations and listen at leisure.

*Spy sets transmission frequency here*

**TELEPHONE TRANSMITTER**
A telephone tap has the advantage that the "target" picks up the microphone and speaks directly and clearly into it! However, the spy hears only telephone calls, not other speech in the room.

*Wiretap is connected directly to line*

**WIRETAP**
Sometimes a phone line can be tapped by connecting a couple of wires to leads in the junction box where the telephone line enters the building.

*Telephone tap connected by clips to a particular line*

*Fibre-optic light-sensing device*

*Flexible antenna broadcasts call to listening spy or recorder*

*Alligator clip connects to telephone line*

*Transmitter*

*Second alligator clip*

*Transmitter*

*Light-sensing device causes transmission to shut down when receiver is replaced*

*Bug powered by lithium is harder to detect than bug that draws power from telephone line*

*Light-sensing device*

*Microprocessor unit picks up signals from light-sensing device and activates transmitter*

Bugged telephone in transparent casing

# Listening in

Bugs do not have a very great range. In a city a spy must position a receiver within 2,625 ft (800 m) of the bug to be sure of good reception. Longer ranges are possible in rural areas, where buildings do not obstruct the signal, and where there is less interference from other radio users. The "listening post" – the receiving station – can be in an adjacent building, in a parked car, or even in the spy's pocket. The bug can be hidden in clothing if an agent has arranged a meeting with a contact in a street or park. Supporting agents listen in with cordless earphones.

*Pin-sized antenna*

*Shirt hides induction loop*

*Receiver can switch between two different bugs*

*Tape runs continually throughout the conversation*

## BUG IN THE EAR

With a "necktie" of wire, an agent can monitor a bug without wearing conspicuous headphones. The listening device fits in the ear and looks like a hearing aid. The wire around the agent's neck creates an induction loop – a magnetic field that relays the amplified signal from a pocket receiver to the ear.

## WEARING A WIRE

The radio signal from a bug hidden in a spy's clothing can alert counter-espionage agents operating bug detection equipment (pp. 48–49). A miniature tape-recorder gets around the problem because it does not broadcast a radio signal.

*Wearer uses remote switch on microphone to turn tape off*

## A BETTER RECEPTION

Though some general-purpose receivers can pick up bug signals, specially designed units are often more convenient and provide better reception. This battery-powered model links up with a portable tape recorder for unattended monitoring. An agent who set it up to receive signals from a telephone tap would need to return to the device only occasionally to change the tapes.

*Telescopic antenna*

*Socket for headphones*

*Car battery can power receiver for extended operation*

MON  CHANNEL  TAPE MANUAL RUN AUTO  TAPE POLARITY + −  BATT LOW  **Lorraine Electronics** LONDON  OFF VOLUME  **UXR3**

*Tape recorder can be hidden in briefcase*

*Tiny tape recorder looks like a personal stereo, but has been modified to provide far better sound quality*

*Bug is only 0.16 in (4 mm) thick, and can hide behind a credit card, or nestle between pages of a diary*

**STAKEOUT**
Hidden microphones are legally used to investigate serious crimes and threats to national security. Here, the head of security for a large American corporation listens in on a suspicious conversation. Laws limit the use of bugs, but some citizens' rights groups fear the controls are too weak.

*Compartments in spine of case conceal the power supply and transmitter electronics*

*Pocket calculator works normally, but broadcasts signal from sensitive microphone even while in use*

*Pen contains tiny bug*

**MAKING A CASE FOR BUGGING**
Monitoring a meeting is a common task for both political and industrial spies. Business-people can have many reasons for recording conversations: tapes can provide evidence of unfair competition or help thwart a takeover by rivals. Bugging a briefcase is a discreet way to make a lasting record of "hush-hush" deals. Microphones built into an attaché case can pick up speech on the far side of a large room. The case can either record the conversation or transmit it to a monitoring device outside. Touching the lock and a brass rivet head at the same time activates the device. A bugged pen or calculator will attract no attention on a desk, and allows a spy to move the microphone nearer to the people talking.

# Dropping in

HOMING PIGEONS have
played an important part
in intelligence work since
the earliest days of espionage.
Carrying a precious cargo of
vital secrets, the homing pigeon
can soar high over enemy
territory. Roman general Julius
Caesar (100–44 B.C.) used them to
send intelligence messages during
his campaigns in what is now France.
Ever since, spies have valued the
pigeon's speed and its ability to return
home in almost any weather. More than
half a million pigeons carried messages
in World War I. Some even worked as
spies – reconnaissance pigeons carried
aloft tiny cameras to photograph enemy
fortifications. In World War II, spies used
pigeons to guide Allied bombers to the
launch sites of the German V1 "flying bombs."

*Strong,*
*lightweight*
*string attaches*
*parachute*
*to bird*

*Parachute made from*
*cotton material*

*Miniature parachute canopy*
*provided soft landing*

### PARACHUTING PIGEON
Britain's SOE (pp. 32–33) dropped
messenger pigeons to spies in
occupied France by parachute.
A special corselet protected the
bird during descent. Agents
collected the pigeons at the drop
zone, and fed and cared for the
birds until they were needed.
This could be difficult. The
pigeons required a lot of care
and spies had to carry them
with them if they went on
long journeys. Some spies
concealed the pigeons in
deep pockets sewn into
their vests. When released
from their temporary
homes, the pigeons flew
back to their lofts in
England with secret
messages in containers
fixed to their legs.

*Lead weights were carefully*
*placed so they did not rattle*

### SMUGGLING GOODS
Airdrops supplied World War I
spies with more than just pigeons
to carry messages home. Money,
weapons, and food all arrived by
parachute, often cleverly disguised.
This ox-tongue can contains a map
of France, a pair of wire cutters, and
several compasses. Lead weights in
the bottom of the can prevented the
tin from feeling unnaturally light.

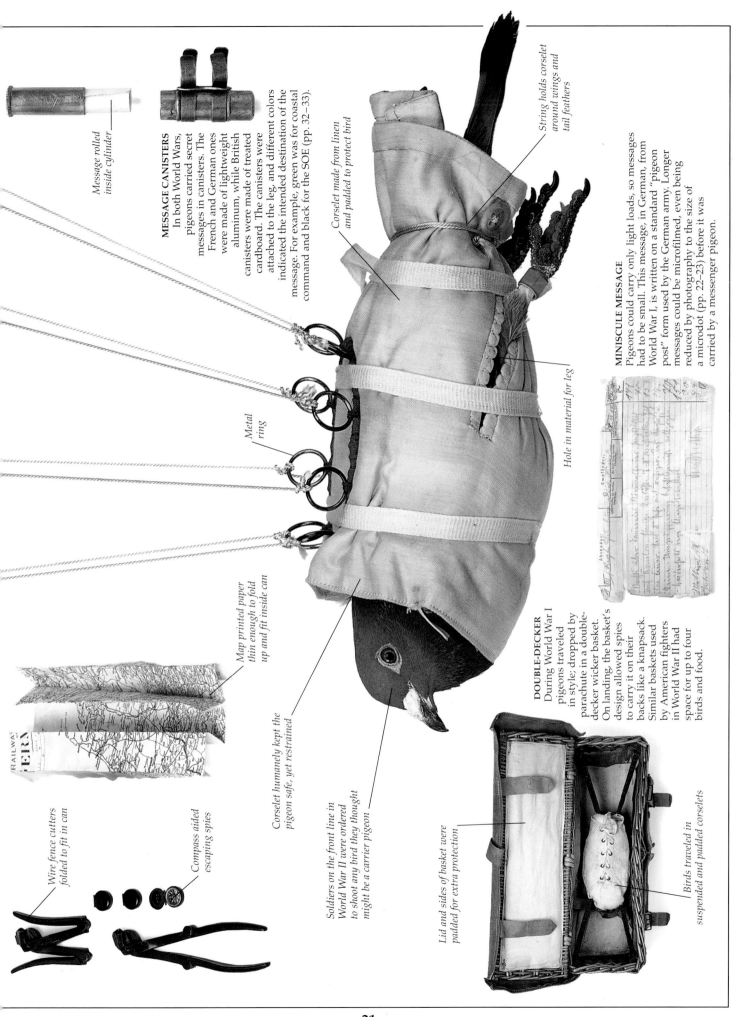

*Message rolled inside cylinder*

**MESSAGE CANISTERS**
In both World Wars, pigeons carried secret messages in canisters. The French and German ones were made of lightweight aluminum, while British canisters were made of treated cardboard. The canisters were attached to the leg, and different colors indicated the intended destination of the message. For example, green was for coastal command and black for the SOE (pp. 32–33).

*String holds corselet around wings and tail feathers*

*Corselet made from linen and padded to protect bird*

*Hole in material for leg*

*Metal ring*

**MINISCULE MESSAGE**
Pigeons could carry only light loads, so messages had to be small. This message, in German, from World War I, is written on a standard "pigeon post" form used by the German army. Longer messages could be microfilmed, even being reduced by photography to the size of a microdot (pp. 22–23) before it was carried by a messenger pigeon.

*Map printed on paper thin enough to fold up and fit inside can*

*Corselet humanely kept the pigeon safe, yet restrained*

*Soldiers on the front line in World War II were ordered to shoot any bird they thought might be a carrier pigeon*

*Wire fence cutters folded to fit in can*

*Compass aided escaping spies*

**DOUBLE-DECKER**
During World War I pigeons traveled in style; dropped by parachute in a double-decker wicker basket. On landing, the basket's design allowed spies to carry it on their backs like a knapsack. Similar baskets used by American fighters in World War II had space for up to four birds and food.

*Lid and sides of basket were padded for extra protection*

*Birds traveled in suspended and padded corselets*

# Secret messages

SPIES RELY ON FAST, secure communications. Speed is crucial because intelligence quickly loses its value, and secrecy is essential to protect both the messages sent and the spy. The invention of radio at the beginning of this century improved the speed of such communications, but not the security. With radios, spies could communicate over long distances almost instantly. However, anyone tuning to the right wavelength was able to intercept radio messages. With two receivers and suitable antennae, counterespionage agents could pinpoint the transmitter in minutes and capture the spy.

Headphones allowed agent to listen to broadcasts without others hearing them

Transmitter works on electricity or battery power

Apparatus packs into a suitcase and weighs 32 lb (14.5 kg)

Oluf Reed Olsen's code sheets

Headphone connector

Frequency dial

Voltage adjuster

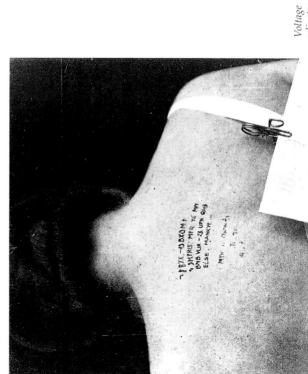

**HUMAN SIGNALS**
Spies sometimes take desperate risks to carry intelligence. This World War I courier carried a message written on her back in invisible ink. The ruse did not succeed: after the captors discovered the message, they executed her.

Spare valve

Crystal plugs in to change transmission frequency

*Terminals attached to car battery for transmission without electrical power*

*Antenna – a 60-ft (18-m) length of wire – plugs in here*

*Spare tubes were carried in this compartment*

*Tapping key sends coded messages as long and short pulses of radio waves*

## NORWEGIAN SECRET AGENT

When German forces invaded neutral Norway in 1940, Oluf Reed Olsen fled the country in a sailboat. Reaching Britain, he trained as a radio operator, returning to Norway in 1943, where spies in the Kristiansand naval base supplied him with details of German shipping movements. Olsen coded the messages and transmitted them to Britain from a camouflaged camp hidden in the trees above the harbor at Kristiansand. He used the radio set shown here. The cipher was considered unbreakable because it was based on sets of random numbers of which Reed Olsen and MI6 held the only copies.

Oluf Reed Olsen using the Mark II suitcase radio at his camouflaged base in 1944

MICRODOTS
Photography provides agents with a simple way to send messages secretly. By photographing a document with a special camera, a spy can produce a microdot – a negative that is 300 times smaller than the original. This paragraph about microdots can be reduced to a microdot the size of a full stop, and then hidden in a perfectly innocent letter. The agent who receives the letter can read every word of the microdot with the help of a microscope.

*Entire message can be reduced until it is the size of a period*

## CONVICTED BY RADIO
Peter and Helen Kroger hid a radio transmitter under the kitchen floor of their house. With it they transmitted British submarine secrets to Russia. They chose a house in west London, England, close to three busy airports, hoping that communications between aircraft and control towers would hide their secret signals. At their trial in 1961, the radio was used as evidence.

## DOTTY PHOTOGRAPHY
Microdot cameras can be simple in construction and small enough to hide easily. However, microphotography is difficult to do. Unless agents are very careful with the exposure of the film and its processing, the dot will be impossible to read.

Microdot camera (actual size)

## MICRODOTS
Photography provides agents with a simple way to send messages secretly. By photographing a document with a special camera, a spy can produce a microdot – a negative that is 300 times smaller than the original. This paragraph about microdots can be reduced to a microdot the size of a period, and then hidden in a perfectly innocent letter. The agent who receives the letter can read every word of the microdot with the help of a microscope.

# Codes and ciphers

ESPIONAGE AGENTS use "codes" to communicate, and "ciphers" to keep their messages secret. In a code, letters, numbers, or symbols replace the words of a message or signal. Some codes are in general use. For example, when you mail a letter, a zip code guides it to the right destination. Spies sometimes send messages in Morse code – dots and dashes that all radio operators understand. Other codes are complicated and difficult to break. Ciphers provide further secrecy. They are similar to codes, but they have a secret "key" for encrypting the message – translating it into a cipher. The key can be a number, a word, even a poem. Anyone who has been given the key can easily decrypt the signal – change it back to plain text. Without knowing the key, the message reads as nonsense.

**SIMPLE CIPHER**
Ciphers do not need to be complicated if it is important only to hide their meaning from a casual glance. This jolly figure from World War I spells out "Ypres" (the site in France of a famous battle) and a date, the "8th."

**CIPHER DISK**
This metal cipher disk, invented in 1802, is less than 2.5 in (6 cm) in diameter. The two inner circles are rotated to align with different letters and numbers on the two outer circles. This produces a simple, easily broken substitution cipher in which each letter stands for another. "W," for example, represents "E" whenever it occurs.

*Code sheet is tiny so Yvonne Cormeau could easily hide it*

**CODE SHEETS**
Charts like these make ciphers easy to write and hard to break. These miniature code sheets were hidden in the purse of SOE wireless operator Yvonne Cormeau in World War II (pp. 32–33). When she used a chart for Morse transmissions, a different letter would replace "E" each time it occurred in the message.

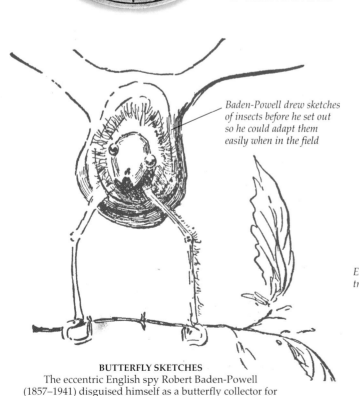

*Baden-Powell drew sketches of insects before he set out so he could adapt them easily when in the field*

**BUTTERFLY SKETCHES**
The eccentric English spy Robert Baden-Powell (1857–1941) disguised himself as a butterfly collector for one of his intelligence-gathering missions in Montenegro, on the coast of the Adriatic Sea. While he was there, he sketched this specimen of a moth perched on a twig.

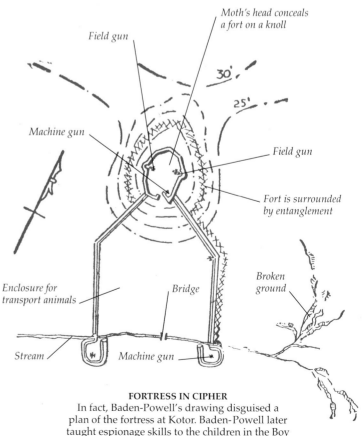

*Moth's head conceals a fort on a knoll*

*Field gun*

*Machine gun*

*30'*

*25'*

*Field gun*

*Fort is surrounded by entanglement*

*Enclosure for transport animals*

*Bridge*

*Broken ground*

*Stream*

*Machine gun*

**FORTRESS IN CIPHER**
In fact, Baden-Powell's drawing disguised a plan of the fortress at Kotor. Baden-Powell later taught espionage skills to the children in the Boy Scout movement, which he founded in 1908.

Numbers between the symbols represented people's names

Coded letter signed by Anthony Babington, conspirator in a plot to assassinate Elizabeth I

### ROYAL CIPHER

Mary, Queen of Scots (1542–87) encrypted messages to allies outside her prison walls (pp. 28–29). In the substitution cipher that they used, the same symbol stood for a letter each time it appeared, so that the cipher was easy to break.

Lid holds spare lightbulbs

Bulbs lit behind lettered windows on the lid to indicate enciphered character

Positions of rotors controlled encryption of each letter

Rotors spun after each letter, ensuring that cipher pattern was never repeated

Cipher was keyed in

Connecting sockets with plugs made the cipher more complicated

Rotors and plugs gave several billion combinations

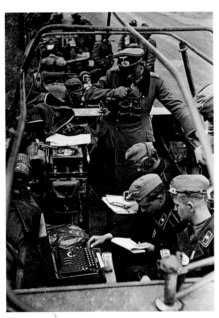

### SPEEDING UP ENCRYPTION

The Enigma cipher machine was used by German soldiers (above), diplomats, and spies in the 1930s and during World War II. The signals baffled enemy cryptanalysts (cipher experts) who intercepted them and tried to break the cipher. The Polish secret service, with the help of a recruited spy in the German cipher office, was able to interpret three-quarters of the Enigma messages by 1938, and in 1939, passed on this knowledge to Britain and France.

### ENIGMA IN OPERATION

After setting plugs and three or four rotors, encryption on Enigma was automatic. Pressing a letter key lit up a different letter on the display above. The encrypted letter was different each time. Decryption on the receiving Enigma machine reversed the process. In principle, coded messages from the Enigma machine were impossible to read without knowing the rotor and plug settings. But that information and an actual Enigma machine supplied by the Polish Secret Service helped the British break most of the Enigma codes in an operation called "Ultra," which remained secret until 1972.

# Intercepts and code-breaking

CIPHERS HELP PROTECT secret messages, but they do not destroy the meaning completely. Like a word puzzle, the sense of the message remains locked inside. An enemy who intercepts the signal will try hard to find the key. Intelligence agencies employ code-breakers called cryptanalysts to do this. With a substitution cipher (pp. 24–25), a cryptanalyst starts by counting letters. In English, "E" is used more often than other letters. So, if in the message "W" appears most, it probably stands for "E." The next step is to look for two-letter words ending in "E." There are only four in English: "he," "me," "be," and "we." Then the cryptanalyst will look for letters that stand on their own – in English there are just two one-letter words, "a" and "I." With techniques like these, and even more complex ones, cryptanalysts can solve elaborate cipher puzzles, although it can sometimes take them a long time. Computers speed the process, but cryptanalysts need to be very patient. Few, though, are as patient as a 17th-century Arab who deciphered a message to the sultan of Morocco. It took him 16 years.

**CIPHER CLERKS AT WORK**
Britain's code-breaking center in World War II was at Bletchley Park near London. More than 5,000 employees there worked on up to 2,000 encrypted messages a day.

**ZIMMERMANN TELEGRAM**
Deciphered in Britain in 1916, this telegram was sent by the Germans to their ambassador in Mexico. It suggested that Mexico form an alliance with Germany and invade three southern U.S. states. The interception of the telegram was possibly the most important spying event of the war. Shocked Americans quickly entered World War I on Britain's side.

*Polish inventors named machine after the ice-cream "bombe" they were eating at the time*

WRENS *(members of the Women's Royal Navy) operated the machines*

**GOING LIKE A BOMBE**
Cryptanalysts at the code-breaking center at Bletchley Park used some of the first computers to help them break codes and ciphers. In two hours, a "bombe" could try every combination of rotor positions that was in use on the simple Enigma machines that Germany was using until 1938. A later machine, called Colossus, was a forerunner of the programmable computers in use today.

*Bombe simply stopped when it broke the cipher*

*The attack was at night and U.S. servicemen were asleep in their bunks*

*Unprepared U.S. technicians thought the Japanese planes were part of a training exercise*

Japanese aircraft bomb Pearl Harbor, December 7, 1941

## THE PURPLE MACHINE
Like Enigma (pp. 24–25), the Japanese Purple cipher machine used a plugboard to create a huge number of possible keys. However, Purple used telephone switches in place of the rotors found in Enigma. A team of U.S. cryptanalysts, including William Friedman (center left), cracked the Purple cipher by building a replica of the mechanism.

## PEARL HARBOR PREDICTED
By cracking the Purple code (right), American cipher experts predicted a Japanese attack on December 7, 1941, but could not name the hour or the place. The spies Richard Sorge (pp. 34–35) and Dusko Popov (pp. 56–57) had also warned of the air attack. American politicians decided to do nothing, and the devastating surprise raid took place on Pearl Harbor in Hawaii. The attack killed 2,300 Americans, crippled the American fleet, and drew the United States into World War II.

## HUSBAND AND WIFE TEAM
Russian-born American William F. Friedman (1891–1969) led the U.S. Army Signals Intelligence Service team that cracked Japan's Purple cipher. Friedman worked on ciphers during both world wars. In the 1920s, his wife Elizebeth broke the codes of rum smugglers during Prohibition, when alcohol was banned in the United States.

*Herbert Yardley's security pass*

## PIONEERING CRYPTANALYST
Herbert Osborne Yardley (1889–1958) was a brilliant cryptanalyst and pioneered code-breaking for the United States during World War I and afterward. He set up the U.S. unit that became known as the "Black Chamber" to read foreign intelligence material. His work in the 1920s was later used to help break the Purple cipher.

## THE "DEAD SOLDIER"
In 1943, the drowned body of a British major washed ashore in Spain. Papers he was carrying described plans by the Allies to attack Greece and Sardinia, and German troops immediately moved there. In fact, "Major Martin" was actually a civilian who had died of pneumonia. Intelligence chiefs had arranged for his body to be dressed as a soldier and pushed from a submarine off the Spanish coast. The Germans were completely fooled, and when they moved their troops, they left very few soldiers on Sicily – the Allies' real target.

*Planted theater ticket stubs to make the major's identity appear genuine*

*"Major Martin's" fake identity card planted by intelligence officers*

*Photograph of living person who looked like "Major Martin"*

**SPY RING**
Microdots (pp. 20–21) reduce documents to the size of a period. In World War II, British agents hid them in this hollow ring.

# Concealment

A CLOAK AND DAGGER are the symbolic trademarks of the secret agent. The spy hides the dagger, the badge of the assassin, under the cloak, which stands for secrecy, disguise, and concealment. Spies of the past could put on a cloak quickly to hide their true identity. Some chose more exotic disguises – Louis XV's agent the Chevalier d'Eon dressed as a woman for many years. For a modern spy, disguise is just as necessary, but much more subtle. Today's agents try to look ordinary, aiming to pass unnoticed in a crowd. Agents also choose ordinary-looking objects as hiding places for their surveillance equipment. Hidden in a working battery, a secret message is safe from even a close inspection. By miniaturizing their messages, spies can conceal them in even smaller objects. Large objects are more difficult to hide. However, an ingenious and determined spy can hide heavy equipment, tank engines – even kidnapped people.

*Wrist strap*

*Right-angle viewfinder*

*Lens*

*Direct vision viewfinder*

*Setting for bright light*

*Aperture setting knob*

**ROYAL BEER BARREL**
Imprisoned by England's Queen Elizabeth I, Mary, Queen of Scots (1542–87) smuggled messages to sympathizers in a beer barrel. She wrapped encrypted documents in a waterproof bag, probably an animal bladder. Then she pushed the bag through the stopper hole into the barrel. Replies traveled back into her prison by the same route. Her "mailman," a double agent named Gilbert Gifford, betrayed the scheme (pp. 42–43).

Mary, Queen of Scots

*Top hides 35 mm film*

**SMILE, PLEASE!**
"Detective" cameras disguised as books, hats, and neckties first appeared in the 1880s. As early as 1893 spies were taking pictures with cameras shaped like pocket watches. This wristwatch camera dates from 1948. On its 1-inch (25-mm) diameter disk of film it takes eight pictures, each the size of a little fingernail.

*Cell provides 1.5 volts power*

*Compartment is big enough to hold a roll of film*

*Magnet grips base to unscrew it*

*Wooden stopper seals barrel when full of beer*

*Spike pushes into ground*

**DEAD LETTER DROP**
Many spies conceal messages in prearranged hiding places, or "dead drops." Leaving a message in a spike at a dead drop is safer than arranging to meet an agent.

**BATTERIES INCLUDED**
This ingenious hiding place looks like a normal battery, and a cell inside provides enough power to light a bulb. However, there is a secret compartment at the base.

Dukes as Comrade
Piotrovsky

Dukes as an ailing
intellectual

Dukes as a bearded
worker

Dukes as an epileptic

Contemporary
print of the
Chevalier d'Eon

*D'Eon complained that
he sometimes forgot
whether he was wearing
a woman's headdress
or a man's helmet*

*People even
made bets on
d'Eon's true sex*

**A RELUCTANT WOMAN**
The Chevalier d'Eon (1728–
1810) was an expert fencer and
lawyer. He began his career as
a spy for French king Louis XV
in 1756. He posed as a shy
woman in the Russian court
to gain the confidence of
the Russian empress,
and also worked as
a double agent for
the British. He
lived in London
as a female at the
end of his life,
and when he died
many people were
shocked to learn
his real identity.

**AGENT ST 25**
Paul Dukes became an expert
in disguise as head of British
intelligence in Russia. He was in
Moscow in 1917 when revolution
swept the Communists to power.
Pursued by the *Cheka* (secret
police), Dukes cheekily
posed as a Comrade
Piotrovsky, a Cheka
officer. To the British,
he was "Agent ST 25."

*Clamps held
ankles and neck*

*Small seat*

**HOW TO SMUGGLE A SPY**
In 1964, drugged and bundled
in a trunk, Israeli Mordecai
Louk narrowly escaped being
exported from Rome to Cairo
disguised as "diplomatic
mail." He was freed when a
customs guard heard the
box whimper. He had
been spying in
Italy for the
Egyptians.

*Leather
slots for feet*

*Trunk was only
53 in (137 cm) long*

# Spies at war

ADVANCING ARMIES rely on expert soldiers to survey the land ahead and judge the enemy's strength. However, not all are spies. Some are scouts who work openly and wear army uniforms. If they are caught, they spend the rest of the war in prison. Spies, on the other hand, disguise themselves to avoid capture, and they collect information secretly. Anyone caught in enemy territory wearing the clothes of a civilian can be tried as a spy, and the punishment – usually execution – is immediate. Despite this harsh penalty, spies have operated in almost every war. The 18th-century German king Frederick the Great even bragged about the number he employed. Mocking a French commander as a gourmet, he joked, "A hundred cooks follow him – but ahead of me go a hundred spies!"

Major Coleridge's diary, July 13, 1899

**SOUTHERN BELLE**
Many women worked as spies in the U.S. Civil War (1861–65), and Belle Boyd (1844–1900) became one of the most famous Confederate (Southern) agents. She learned military secrets from Union (Northern) officers lodged in her Virginia home, and braved gunfire to tell Confederate leaders. After capture and then release in a prisoner exchange, she received a hero's welcome in the South.

**DETECTIVE SPYMASTER**
When civil war divided the United States, President Abraham Lincoln turned to a private detective to help gather intelligence for the Union army. The choice seemed a natural one – the Scotsman Allan Pinkerton (1819–84), head of the famous agency, had already foiled one attempt to assassinate Lincoln. Unfortunately, Pinkerton knew little about war, and his agents were clumsy and sometimes cowardly. He resigned as Lincoln's spymaster in 1862.

**DEATH OF A SPY**
Major John André, above, (1750–80) was hanged as a spy during the American Revolution (1775–83). He had gone to meet American traitor Benedict Arnold (1741–1801), the commander of West Point, a fortress that guarded the Hudson River Valley. Arnold wanted to surrender the fort to the British, and he handed André details of his plans. The ship that was to take André and the secret plans back to the British army was fired upon and left without him. André disguised himself as a civilian but was caught by American militia with the secret papers in his boots.

*Hollow bullet used by Major Coleridge to hide his messages*

## FIGHTING THE BOERS

In the Boer War (1899–1902), British forces fought to control farms and gold in what is now South Africa. Their enemies were the Afrikaners, or Boers, descendants of white Dutch settlers. Major H. F. Coleridge was among those who spied for the British, and his diaries (left) record details of the Boer defenses. The British intelligence service did not realize the value of the intelligence that spies like Coleridge supplied, and he had to plead for more money to continue his work (below).

### CARTOON CAPTURE

During World War I (1914–18), spies usually operated far from the front line, in neutral nations such as Switzerland and the Netherlands (Holland). Nevertheless, the public fear of spies and their exploits inspired many cartoons. This colorful example shows a German spy captured by French troops.

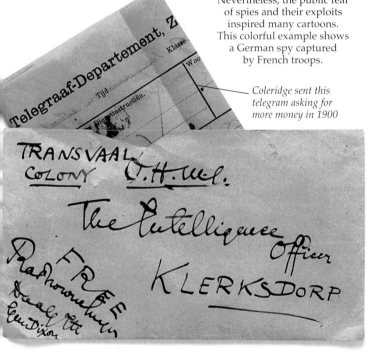

*Coleridge sent this telegram asking for more money in 1900*

*French-born Violette Szabo was the best shot in Britain's SOE*

### COURAGEOUS COMMANDO

Violette Szabo's only qualification when she applied to be a British spy in World War II (1939–45) was her skill with a rifle – London shooting galleries banned her because she always hit the target. She became a spy to avenge the death of her husband, Etienne (above), who died fighting for the British in North Africa. Admired by fellow spies for her courage and determination, she was captured after a gun battle on her second SOE (Special Operations Executive) mission in France, when she was sabotaging telegraph lines. Violette Szabo was executed in a German prison camp.

*Lincoln (center) also dismissed his general*

*On September 17, 1862, 12,000 Union troops died at the battle of Antietam, largely due to bad intelligence, and Pinkerton resigned*

### TOO GOOD TO BE TRUE

The cleverest agent of World War II, code-named "Cicero," was extremely good at spying for Germany. He was an Albanian and his real name was Elyesa Bazna. While working as valet to the British ambassador in Turkey, he opened the embassy safe and photographed secret codes, lists of British spies, and the Allied plans to invade Europe. But these documents were so secret that the German leaders could not believe they were genuine and ignored Cicero. Nevertheless, they paid him a fortune in banknotes – but all of them were forgeries.

# A cover story

**BITTER PILL**
All SOE agents carried a suicide L-pill, which would kill in five seconds. No agent ever used it.

Disguised as a child's nurse, "Annette" passes through a wartime roadblock in southwest France. Annette, who is really the radio operator Yvonne Cormeau, tells her "cover story" well, escaping capture for a year and transmitting more than 400 coded messages. During World War II, the lives of many secret agents depended on their cover stories – invented pasts designed to hide their real identity. In Britain, the Special Operations Executive (SOE) gave trained agents cover stories that they learned by heart. Then the SOE dropped the agents in France by parachute or small boat.

Fake French matchbox

**FOR DEFENSE**
Male and female agents learned techniques of silent killing, and all carried knives to put the techniques into practice if necessary.

**VITAL TIMING**
A late arrival usually signaled danger. Cautious agents did not wait more than a few minutes at a rendezvous.

**PARTING GIFT**
SOE agents were given a valuable present such as this silver cigarette case before leaving on a mission. The gift could be used as a bribe if an agent was caught by a corrupt official.

Wallet

Powder compact

**MAPS**
Agents used local maps to plan sabotage. A silk map (above) folds very small to aid concealment.

*Mirror*

**TINY TAPPER**
A Morse code key was small enough to hide easily in a handbag.

**PLUG-IN TUNING**
Yvonne Cormeau carried a variety of crystals. She could change them to tune her SOE radio to the correct wavelength.

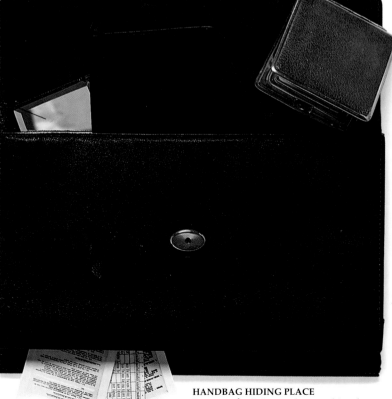

*Code sheets*

**HANDBAG HIDING PLACE**
Between the lining and outer skin of Yvonne Cormeau's handbag is the secret compartment in which she hid code sheets (pp. 24–25) and a transmission schedule.

The clothes had to be tailored in the French style of the 1940s

SOE carefully removed all English labels before sending an agent into enemy territory

Every detail of clothing reinforced the cover story – an agent posing as a clerk would wear a simple, inexpensive hat like this one

Yvonne Cormeau's battered leather briefcase

Briefcase fitted in with one of Yvonne Cormeau's disguises – a district nurse

Yvonne Cormeau's dress was made from lightweight cotton

Stockings could be used as a bribe by the SOE agent, as silk was very rare in wartime

Suede shoes

**YVONNE CORMEAU, SOE RADIO OPERATOR**
Many of these items belonged to Yvonne Cormeau, the SOE agent whose cover name was Annette. She parachuted into France on the night of August 22, 1943 and worked as a radio operator. Her natural caution helped her avoid capture until Allied forces liberated France in 1944. On one occasion, she recognized another agent on a train but resisted the temptation to speak – she had learned in training that if he was under suspicion, they might both be captured. On the other hand, Yvonne Cormeau knew when it was worth taking a risk. Although most radio operators moved their radio sets daily to avoid capture, she felt safe transmitting from the same house for six months. From the windows she could spot interception vans over 3 miles (5 km) away.

# Double agents and defectors

D OUBLE AGENTS ARE REALLY "controlled enemy agents." Rather than serving two masters they work for only one side in a war of espionage – but they deceive the other side into thinking they are working for them, and instead steal their secrets. Being a double agent is very risky. To be successful, they must develop the trust of an intelligence agency, while their sole aim is to betray that trust. If caught, they can expect no mercy in their punishment. Double agents may be volunteers, or they could be spies unmasked by counterintelligence agencies who have been "turned" (recruited and controlled) rather than prosecuted. Spies who are turned are especially valuable. Their new masters provide them with false but believable information, and the spy passes on the bogus secrets as if they were true, causing confusion and doubt. Spies who flee to the nation that was once the target of their spying are called "defectors." Although they may be admired in the country to which they are truly loyal, they earn just as much hatred in the country they betrayed.

**TRIBUTE TO A SPY**
Richard Sorge (1895–1944) appeared to be a fanatical Nazi during World War II. While a political adviser to the German ambassador, he was feeding secrets to Germany's Russian enemies. Soviet stamps showed Sorge as a hero.

**A TRAITOR'S DEATH**
Japanese counterespionage agents unmasked Richard Sorge for their German allies. He was condemned and executed in 1944.

Aldrich and Rosario Ames after their separate trials for spying

**ANCIENT SPYMASTER**
Chinese commander Sun Tzu was among the first to write about double agents. He called them "doomed spies," who "are deliberately given false information and told to report it to the enemy." Sun Tzu wrote his book, *The Art of War*, in the 4th century B.C.

**RUSSIAN AGENT AT THE CIA**
For nine years Aldrich Ames (born 1941) was a Soviet spy while working as a trusted officer at the CIA. Ames and his wife, Rosario, provided details of many spies recruited by the CIA, and with their help, Moscow was able to build a network of double agents who deceived their CIA bosses. The pair was paid well by the Russians for their treachery.

# ЗДРАВСТВУЙТЕ, ТОВАРИЩ ФИЛБИ

«Если бы мне предстояло начать жизнь сызнова, я начал бы так, как начал».

Феликс ДЗЕРЖИНСКИЙ.

ДЕКАБРЬСКОЕ морозное утро, ночная мгла еще не ушла с заснеженных улиц. Деревья на Гоголевском бульваре покрыты пушистым инеем. У троллейбусной остановки — цепочка по-

представить все, что угодно. Предположить, что в то августовское утро в кабинете за столом напротив него сидел кадровый сотрудник советской разведки, он не мог даже в дурном сне.

— Я делал, что мог в то время, и был счастлив узнать однажды, что я зачислен в кадры советской разведки.
— Каким же образом, товарищ Ким, вам удалось попасть на службу в английскую разведку?
— Это довольно длинная история, — говорит он. — После окончания Кэмбриджа я некоторое время работал в одной

— Я пошел вверх по служебной лестнице. Через год я уже был заместителем начальника одного из отделов МИ-5.
— МИ-6, что это значит?
— В Англии существует две службы: под кодовым названием МИ-5 скрывается контрразведка, МИ-6 — это собственно секретная разведывательная служба.
— Западная пресса отмечала, что ва-

Он был внимателен в обращении с людьми, но по существу относился к ним свысока. В дела он не вникал, и, я бы сказал, при всей его агрессивности он был дилетантом, о чем лучше всего говорит авантюра с вторжением на Кубу тех позорно провалившимся. Считали, что он занял этот пост благодаря своему брату — Джону Фостеру Даллесу

### HERO'S WELCOME
Philby escaped to Moscow from Beirut, where he had been working under cover as a journalist. The Soviet newspapers welcomed him with banner headlines. This one reads "Greetings, Comrade Philby."

*Hammer and sickle, the symbol of the Soviet Union*

### COLD WAR DOUBLE AGENT
Harold "Kim" Philby (1912–88) became a Communist while he was studying at Cambridge University, and was a Soviet spy by 1933. Yet, seven years later he had a job with Britain's MI6 intelligence service. After thirty years of spying, he fled to Moscow. A grateful Soviet Union gave him a pension and an apartment, the office of which is shown above.

### MEDALS FROM BOTH SIDES
Philby received this KGB badge soon after his arrival in Moscow. Later the Soviet Union awarded him the Order of the Red Banner. Eighteen years earlier, England's King George VI, unaware that he was a spy, had given Kim the Order of the British Empire.

### RETIREMENT IN MOSCOW
After defecting, Philby lived in Moscow until his death in 1988. His son took this photograph of him in the 1970s. The treachery of Philby and his fellow spies Guy Burgess and Donald Maclean left behind a trail of mistrust. Their espionage discredited the British intelligence services.

### SECURITY SECRETS
As head of the KGB mission in London, Oleg Gordievsky (born 1939) had access to the most sensitive information about his country's espionage activities. Secretly he despised the Soviet system and had been spying for the West since 1966. He defected to Britain in 1985, when his Soviet masters began to suspect him.

*Gordievsky wrote memoirs of his time in the KGB*

### SECRET IDENTITY
Igor Gouzenko (1919–82) was a cipher clerk in the Soviet embassy in Ottawa. He did not wish to return to the Soviet Union, and defected with evidence of ongoing Soviet spying. He was turned away as a crank by newspapers and government departments, but the Mounted Police believed and protected him. For this TV interview he wore a hood to keep his identity secret.

Gordievsky with his book, *KGB: The Inside Story*

# Secret weapons

Espionage has a bloody past. Spies were busiest in wartime, when there was danger everywhere; and when war ended, it was the job of intelligence organizations to make sure peace continued. Sometimes they used weapons to achieve this peacetime aim, and many wartime spies carried weapons openly. Others disguised their guns and knives in often ingenious ways. With the Cold War (pp. 38–39) came greater secrecy. Both Warsaw Pact and Western powers attempted killings, and some, like the murder of Georgi Markov, succeeded. Other schemes did not: apparently the CIA twice tried, and failed, to kill Cuba's president Fidel Castro with poison. The agency also considered more unusual weapons. They plotted to put deadly bacteria in Castro's cigar and to blow him up with an exploding clam while he swam in the sea. But not all the agency's weapons would have been fatal. The strangest plot just aimed to humiliate the Communist leader. By sprinkling a chemical powder in Castro's shoes, CIA agents planned to make his famous beard fall out!

*Pushing the trigger near the handle fired the pellet*

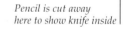

**DEADLY PENCIL**
Disguised as pencils, these two weapons were used in close combat. The stabbing pencil contains a cross-shaped blade, and the propelling pencil fired a single chromium-plated bullet. Agents of Britain's SOE (pp. 32–33) used them to gain a brief advantage, so that they could seize more powerful weapons from their opponents.

*Pencil is cut away here to show knife inside*

*Gun has no barrel, limiting accuracy*

Georgi Markov in 1978

*Shortened barrel*

Modified Webley & Scott 6.35 mm pistol

*Trigger guard*

**UMBRELLA KILLER**
Bulgarian Georgi Markov broadcast criticism of his country's leadership from London. Walking home along a London street one day in 1978, Markov felt a sharp pain. He looked around to see a man picking up an umbrella. Markov quickly developed a fever and died three days later. His assassin, a Bulgarian agent, had used a specially designed umbrella to fire a tiny pellet containing a powerful poison into Markov. Ten days earlier, Bulgarian agents in Paris had attacked another opponent of the country's rulers, but the victim recovered.

*Gas cylinder made umbrella work like air rifle*

*Holes in tiny pellet contained poison*

**GUN BELT**
Worn on a belt under clothing, this small World War II pistol had a very short range. To be sure of a direct hit, an assassin needed to be standing right next to the target. A firing cable from the belt's buckle passed down the sleeve of the coat that covered the gun. The great advantage was that a spy could pull the trigger without anyone seeing him or her take aim or fire.

## SIMPLE SLASHERS
Not all weapons were aimed at people. These razor-sharp knives were designed to destroy vehicle tires. They were small enough to hide easily, yet with a single slash an agent could gain valuable minutes in which to make an escape. Saboteurs used the knives to completely immobilize a vehicle by slashing all the tires (including the spare).

*Knife hung from thong around neck*

*Small slasher resembles ring*

## RING REVOLVER
Concealed weapons are nothing new. The well-equipped French spy of the 19th century carried this tiny revolver fixed to a ring. By revolving the chamber, the agent could fire five shots. Because of its small size and firing method, this design was sometimes called a squeezer pistol or palm pistol.

*Because the pistol is so small, it had a very limited range*

*The ring gun can fire five bullets*

## LETHAL GLOVE
Some spies' weapons appear more dangerous to the person using them than to the victim. An agent firing this ingenious "glove" pistol had to take careful aim, as its single bullet could easily take off a couple of fingers. The U. S. Office of Naval Intelligence produced the gun for its World War II agents.

*Barrel poked out between fingers*

*Pistol is riveted to a leather glove*

*Pressing the barrel against the victim's body fired the gun*

*Canadian maple leaf*

*Concealed blade*

*French tricolor*

*Concealed blade*

## HEEL AND COIN BLADES
Despite their vicious appearance, knives hidden in shoe heels were not intended for attack. Instead, the concealed blades allowed agents who were tied up to cut themselves free. Spies also hid knives in low-denomination coins. They hoped that enemy guards would let them keep their loose change in their pockets – even if the guards stole the paper money.

*Concealed blade*

*Coin has a hidden blade*

## MESSY KNIVES
Wartime intelligence agencies designed these knives so they could be hidden in a coat lapel or cuff. A captured agent could use a knife to attack guards and escape. Instructors who trained the spies warned that the results were often "messy."

# The Cold War

When World War II ended in 1945, the future looked bleak for secret agents. However, a golden age of espionage was about to begin. A political boundary split Europe in two. Nicknamed the "Iron Curtain," it was actually just a line on a map. To the east lay the Communist world – the Soviet Union and its allies – who wanted to create a classless society that shared everything. Nations to the west, supported by the United States, were capitalist, believing in the private ownership of property and businesses. Eastern and Western nations were deeply suspicious of each other, and their rivalry became known as the Cold War. Spies thrived in the atmosphere of mistrust that the Cold War created. They had plenty of work, with East and West racing to construct the biggest bombs, and each side sending spies to discover what the other side was plotting. And because of all this activity, each side needed more spies at home to catch enemy agents at work. On both sides of the Iron Curtain, fear of nuclear war meant that the money for spying never ran out. Finally, in 1989, the Cold War ended, and the process of reuniting Germany, which had also been split in two, began.

**HUNT THE MISSILE**
Missile bases are easy to spot on photographs from spy satellites (pp. 52–53), so the United States and the Soviet Union developed submarine-based missile launchers that could hide beneath the waves. The designers of this Trident missile claimed it would be used to hit missile bunkers. Opponents believed that cities would be the real targets.

*Distinctive mushroom-shaped cloud*

**TESTING THE BOMB**
The United States tested its atom bombs in the Nevada desert, far from the prying eyes of enemy spies. The power of these bombs to destroy civilization frightened everyone and may have gone a long way toward ensuring that neither side in the Cold War actually used one.

*Crowds cheered as everyone with a hammer and chisel chipped at the wall*

**"KEEPING THE WORLD SAFE"**
Politicians during the Cold War believed in "mutually assured destruction" (MAD). If each side had enough bombs to destroy the other, they reasoned, neither side would dare risk war. The two "superpowers," the Soviet Union and the United States, each built huge missiles with nuclear warheads. They never launched them. These American Titan II missiles are in storage, waiting to be converted into satellite launchers.

**THE WALL DIVIDING EUROPE**
Cold War espionage was most intense in Berlin, the capital of East Germany. Berlin was situated well inside East Germany, but a wartime treaty gave France, Britain, and the United States control of West Berlin, so the city was itself divided into West and East. To prevent refugees from escaping to the West across the new border, the East Germans divided the city of Berlin with a wall in 1961. The destruction of the wall in 1989 united Germany and symbolized the end of the Cold War.

## EUROPE DIVIDED

In the Cold War, only four European nations were neutral. Most others signed pacts vowing to defend their neighbors. The Warsaw Pact united Communist countries with the Soviet Union. Capitalist countries were allied with the United States as members of the North Atlantic Treaty Organization (NATO).

## BERLIN SPY SWAP

Any captured Cold War spies could expect execution or, at best, a long spell in jail – unless their government could negotiate a prisoner exchange. Under these deals, East and West swapped captured spies. The released agents walked to freedom at one of the checkpoints along the Berlin Wall.

## SHOT DOWN

Before satellites simplified spying from above the ground, the United States sent U-2 spy planes (pp. 52–53) to photograph the other side of the Iron Curtain. The Soviet Union shot one down in 1960 and captured the CIA spy pilot Gary Powers. He did not have to serve the ten-year sentence because the Soviets freed him in 1962 in exchange for Soviet spy Rudolph Abel.

U-2 pilot Gary Powers pictured after being shot down in 1960

Iron Curtain

Neutral countries

Other capitalist nations

Full NATO members

Other Communist nations

Warsaw Pact

Soviet Union

*Graffiti added to remains of wall after reunification*

# Spymasters

INTELLIGENCE CHIEFS HAVE enormous influence. Their access to valuable and secret information means that the few chiefs who choose not to serve their country wisely have dangerous powers. Usually chiefs, or spymasters, take orders from a trusted government group, but often this group does not know what the spies are really doing. In the past, spymasters in Europe received their orders directly from the king or queen. However, in 1519 a Venetian diplomat wrote of the English king Henry VIII's first spymaster, Cardinal Wolsey, that he "rules both king and the entire kingdom." In this century, until the Cold War ended, secret service chiefs controlled whole Eastern European nations. J. Edgar Hoover's powers grew so great while he was the FBI chief that he was in a position to blackmail some of the most influential politicians in the United States. Countries are now more open about the existence of their security services, but the identity of agents in the spy networks is still a closely guarded secret.

**ROMAN SOLDIER**
General Scipio Africanus Major (236–184 B.C.) was among the most clever spymasters of the Roman Empire. While attacking the Spanish city of Carthago Nova, his spies discovered that the enemy's reinforcements were ten days' march away. As a result, the army and navy under Scipio's leadership won an easy victory.

**POWER BEHIND THE THRONE**
Cardinal Wolsey (1475–1530) became the most powerful man in England as the first head of intelligence services for King Henry VIII. Wolsey's agents opened the mail sent to diplomats from Venice and other nations. To protect their secrets, the ambassadors began to write their letters in code.

Wolsey had influence over the powerful Henry VIII for many years

**INDIAN INTELLIGENCE**
Mughal ruler Akbar (1542–1605) united India. As a young king, he used fakirs (holy men) as spies. During his reign (1556–1605), Akbar extended the Indian empire and reformed the government. To do this he relied on intelligence reports provided by *kotwal* (local officials), who had a duty to employ spies.

**INVISIBLE SPIES**
The warring princes of 12th-century Japan used ninja as spies and silent assassins. The ninja got their name from the Japanese word meaning "to make yourself invisible." They were trained to high standards of fitness and were masters of disguise. One warlord, Takeda Shingen, so feared them that he fitted a second door to his bathroom to make escape easier.

**RUSSIAN SECRET SERVICE**
The first Tsar of Russia, Ivan IV (1530–1584), richly deserved his nickname "the Terrible." He ruled with the help of ruthless secret agents called the *Oprichniki*. Officially security police, the Oprichniki were really thugs who terrorized whole cities, killing and torturing without fear of punishment. They wore an emblem of a dog's head and a broom, symbolizing their power to sniff out and sweep away treason.

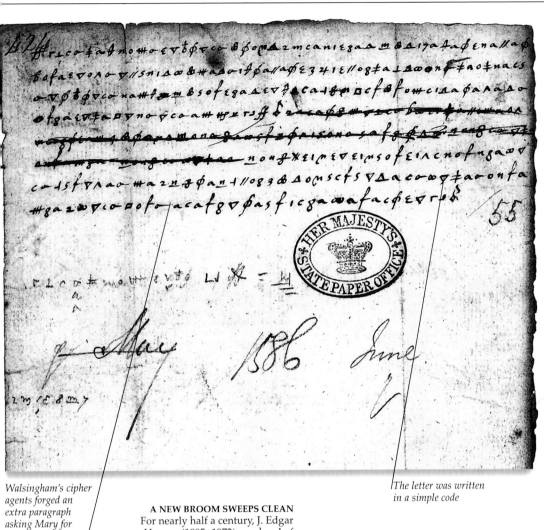

*Walsingham's cipher agents forged an extra paragraph asking Mary for the plotters' names*

*The letter was written in a simple code*

## FATHER OF THE SECRET SERVICE

Francis Walsingham (c. 1532–1590) did much to build up the English intelligence service. His greatest achievement was to uncover a plot to murder England's queen, Elizabeth I. Walsingham's agents intercepted coded letters between the plotters and the queen's imprisoned cousin, Mary, Queen of Scots. The letters proved that Mary was involved, and she was executed in February 1587.

## A NEW BROOM SWEEPS CLEAN

For nearly half a century, J. Edgar Hoover (1895–1972) was head of the FBI, which was formed to detect enemy spies at work in the United States. But Hoover's agents also snooped on the private lives of politicians, including the president. By threatening to make sordid secrets public, Hoover clung to his enormous power. In 1947, the CIA was formed to deal with foreign security, and the power of the FBI was curbed.

## THE RED CARDINAL

Cardinal Richelieu (1585–1642) organized the Cabinet Noir, a secret police force in France. His men spied on noble families, giving Louis XIII more power. The spies gained a reputation – every French teacher of sword-fighting was thought to be an agent.

## DOUBLE AGENT AT THE TOP

Alfred Redl (1846–1913) was Austria's chief spycatcher. He modernized the Austrian Secret Service but ran up huge personal debts. When Russia offered him money for vital information, he accepted and worked with them for ten years. Redl was accused of being a traitor in 1913 and shot himself rather than stand trial.

## WOLF IN SHEEP'S CLOTHING

"The man without a face" was Markus Wolf's nickname during the Cold War. He was in charge of foreign operations for East Germany's Stasi (secret police). Wolf managed highly effective spy rings in the West. Even one of the close aides of the West German chancellor, Willy Brandt (b. 1913), had been recruited and was a Stasi spy.

# The secret services

BEHIND EVERY SPY is a vast network for gathering intelligence. Organizations like the CIA and MI6 give spies documents, money, and help, and interpret the intelligence that the spies collect. The intelligence networks analyze information not only from human spies but also from a host of other sources. Satellites provide some of their data, and interception of radio signals supplies more. Many of their staff do nothing but read foreign newspapers, magazines, and journals. A clever analyst can learn much from these "open sources." During World War II, Russian intelligence experts noticed the United States was hoarding silver for "scientific research," and had banned all atomic physics journals. Without putting agents' lives at risk, they guessed – correctly – that the United States was developing an atom bomb.

**BEWARE OF SPIES**
The Republic of China has a large but highly secretive intelligence network. There is a Central Control of Intelligence that collects information, relying on different government organizations as well as the ordinary person in the street. In the 1970s, plaques such as this one (left) were posted all over the country to warn citizens against the activities of spies. Outside China, spies are believed to operate through the country's embassies and the New China News Agency.

*Message reads: "At all times protect {our} secrets {and} everywhere guard against spies"*

Emblem of the CIA

**GUARDIANS OF THE UNITED STATES**
The Central Intelligence Agency (CIA) has collected and analyzed foreign intelligence for the United States since 1947. It is also responsible for counterintelligence abroad. The less well-known National Security Agency, which is under the control of the Federal Bureau of Investigation (FBI), is actually bigger than the CIA and handles signal intelligence – codes, ciphers, and the interception of communications. A separate organization, the U.S. Secret Service, has responsibility for protecting the president.

Badge of MI5, the counterespionage agency in Britain

**THE STASI**
Until East and West Germany were reunited in 1990, the Stasi (State Security) controlled espionage for the East. East Germans had good reason to fear the Stasi. It employed more than 85,000 people and had detailed files on a third of the population.

*Copy camera with Stasi insignia*

**SECURITY STAR**
Britain has twin security agencies to handle intelligence and counterintelligence at home (MI5) and abroad (MI6). In 1992, Britain was the first country to appoint a woman, Stella Rimington, as the head of a major intelligence agency. Until 1995, she was director of MI5, also called the Security Service, and originally formed in 1906. MI6 is the military name for the Secret Intelligence Service, and staff refer to its shadowy director as "C."

Map showing
the Soviet Union

Badge worn by
a KGB agent

## ISRAELIS SPYING ABROAD

Israel has developed ruthlessly
efficient security and intelligence
services. Formed in 1949,
Mossad (the Institution for
Intelligence and Special
Services) is responsible
for foreign espionage
and taking action
against the country's
enemies. Shin Beth
(Security and
Counterespionage
Service) handles
internal security.

A menorah – the
symbol of Judaism

Badge of Mossad

Vanunu's desperate message about
his kidnapping in Rome

## MOSSAD AT WORK

Agents of Mossad are
particularly skilled at
undercover work in foreign
countries. When Mordechai
Vanunu, a senior Israeli
nuclear technician, revealed
that Israel was building atom
bombs, Mossad agents
kidnapped him in Italy and
took him back to Israel to
face trial and imprisonment.
While in Israeli custody,
Vanunu wrote a message for
the press on his hand, giving
details of the kidnapping.

## SPYING
## IN RUSSIA

The KGB (Committee
of State Security) controlled
intelligence and counter-
intelligence both inside the Soviet
Union and overseas from 1954 until
the 1980s. KGB agents also handled
internal security, and the head of the
organization had immense political
influence. With the birth of modern
Russia, the duties of the KGB
were transferred to less
powerful organizations
in the new republics.

## TARGET PRACTICE

The secret intelligence organizations
of all countries deny that their agents
carry out political killings. However,
history proves this is not true. The CIA
was famous for the actions it took
against foreign leaders who opposed
the United States – they hired Mafia
killers to try and assassinate Cuba's
Communist president, Fidel Castro
(pp. 36–37). And the KGB defector
Oleg Gordievsky claims that the KGB
provided the poisoned umbrella that
killed Georgi Markov (pp. 36–37).

Manurhin
7.65 mm
pistol

## PROTECTING FRANCE

Like many other nations, France divides its
intelligence work among several organizations.
The Direction Générale de la Sécurité Extérieure
(DGSE) collects foreign intelligence and organizes
counterintelligence abroad. The efficient Direction
de la Surveillance du Territoire (DST) is controlled
by the Ministry of the Interior and handles internal
security. In the early 1980s, the DST was directly
responsible for the expulsion of 47 Soviet
diplomats suspected of spying.

DGSE agents abroad defend
themselves with automatics like this

# Surveillance at work

Spies may be watching you. Business secrets are potentially valuable to rival companies, and to obtain those secrets, subterfuge is often used by employees or outside agencies. To steal documents, industrial spies use the tools and methods of a secret agent, and in order to protect those documents from snoopers, businesses must adopt counterespionage tactics (pp. 48–49). The devices shown here could all be used to protect office secrets against intruders. However, all of them can also monitor employees, for the espionage threat may come from inside the company. Workplace spies watch low-paid staff who may be bribed to sell information to rivals. They aim to catch disgruntled managers erasing computer disks. Even office gossip is a target for hidden microphones: it may warn that staff members plan to leave and set up in competition.

**ARE YOU RECEIVING ME?**
Businesspeople can learn a lot about their clients with a tiny bug like this. A sales representative making a presentation can "accidentally" leave a bugged folder in the conference room to record a client's private conversation.

**TAKING PICTURES**
Professional spies might use an expensive camera like this Minox to photograph information. However, the office photocopier is more of a security threat. Employees do not arouse suspicion if they use it – and the copies cost them nothing.

**BUGGING THE WORKPLACE**
An office appliance such as a fluorescent desk lamp is an ideal hiding place for bugs (above). It has a built-in power supply and it sits in the middle of the desk, so it is well placed to pick up conversations. Bribing someone to insert the bug when equipment is sold is less risky than entering the office to plant it.

*With a cheap modem, spies can hack into insecure computer networks and copy data files*

*Base of desk lamp is large enough to conceal bug*

*Shredded paper*

**LOUD AND CLEAR**
A sales representative who has planted a bug is able to eavesdrop on his client from a car parked outside. By pulling up the radio antenna, he can pick up the signal and listen to any discussion of the sales pitch. The following day, the sales rep can return to negotiations, able to use the information to change strategy, and in a better position to bargain.

**PINHOLE PEEPER**
More than one in every ten
American companies use video
cameras to spy on their employees.
Concealing the cameras is simple:
the smallest have lenses that are
smaller than a match head.

**CAUGHT ON CAMERA**
FBI agents used a hidden video camera in 1979
to collect evidence in a corruption case that they
nicknamed "ABSCAM." The video (above) proved
that members of the U.S. Congress were taking
bribes. Seven members of Congress were
convicted and went to jail.

**INFINITY RECEIVER**
Most office bugs have a limited range, but
infinity receivers use the telephone lines to
allow eavesdropping from any telephone in
the world. The "spy" must first install the
device, usually attached to the telephone
line. The bug operates when the spy dials
the number of the bugged telephone, then
presses a specially selected key on a touch-
tone telephone. The bug detects the tone
and stops the target phone from ringing.
Then it allows the spy to hear a
conversation in the room, with the
telephone mouthpiece acting as
a microphone. With the infinity
receiver, it is possible for someone in
Sydney, Australia, to eavesdrop on
conversations in Washington, D.C.

*Screwheads
on clock can
conceal camera*

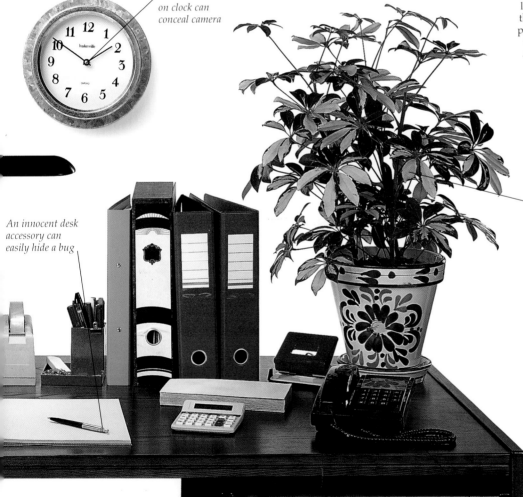

*An innocent desk
accessory can
easily hide a bug*

*Tiny transmitters can
be hidden anywhere –
even in potted plants*

**BUG IN A PLUG**
Disguised as a wall socket, a bug is
impossible to detect without taking
the socket apart or using special
equipment. The socket functions
normally and also supplies the bug
with power. Some devices work like
baby alarms, using the mains power
cables – instead of radio waves – to
transmit signals. The spy monitors
any conversations with a suitable
receiver plugged into any other
socket on the same circuit.

*Infinity tape storage (above) records
phone calls and plays them back
when the "spy" dials in*

**TALKING RUBBISH**
Cutting up documents does
not necessarily destroy them.
Determined industrial spies
can painstakingly piece
together shredded secrets.

# Industrial espionage

GOVERNMENTS AND POLITICIANS are not the only targets of espionage. Businesses also have secrets that industrial spies try to steal or copy. This kind of espionage is rapidly expanding, but it is hardly new. The silk industry was an early victim. Until the 6th century, only the Chinese knew how to make this luxurious cloth. Then the Byzantine emperor Justinian I (483–565) used espionage to steal the secret of its production. He encouraged two monks to smuggle silkworms out of China in hollow canes. Industrial spying is more sophisticated today, but governments still encourage it if their nation benefits. In 1989, the French Department of Commerce planned to steal trade secrets from American and British companies. The spying became public when an informer mailed their "shopping list" to the CIA. Usually, though, it is businesses that use industrial espionage against their competitors. Successful spies find design details, lists of suppliers and buyers. Even advance knowledge of a price list can help squeeze a competitor out of business.

**SPYING ON THE COMPETITION**
One of the most common forms of industrial espionage is for trusted employees to quit and join a competitor – taking secrets with them. General Motors (GM) suspected José Ignacio Lopez de Arriortua of doing this when he left to join their rival Volkswagen. GM claimed that de Arriortua and other executives stole thousands of photographs and plans of the Opel Vectra, which was then secret. The car is now on the market.

*Computer-aided designs of new cars are fiercely protected from industrial espionage*

General Motors' Opel Vectra

*In the U.S. and Canada, annual losses in software, audio-tapes, and videos are $3.131 billion*

*Long before they emerge on the catwalk, designs of evening dresses are the target of spies*

## THE ENTERTAINMENT INDUSTRY

Piracy (illegal copying) and industrial espionage cut the profits made by people in the world of entertainment. From a single original, pirates can make millions of CDs or videos. Security at recording and film studios must be intense to make sure that master tapes are protected until the scheduled release date. Despite these precautions, industrial spies occasionally succeed in smuggling out a recording: pirates in Singapore made thousands of video copies of the James Bond film *A View to a Kill* and distributed them throughout Asia before the film's London première.

*To keep the shape of a new car secret, it can be disguised by fitting new parts in old car bodies when being road-tested*

*Revolutionary disk braking systems may interest rival car manufacturers*

## COSTUME DRAMA

Theft of ideas and designs in the fashion industry is big business. It is easy to claim and often difficult to prove. Cutters and other workers in the garment trade might copy patterns and sell them to another designer. It is also possible to re-create designs from sketches or photographs taken at designer dress shows.

## INDUSTRIAL DIAMONDS

An industrial spy at General Electric earned $1 million a year for passing secrets of synthetic diamond manufacture to a South Korean company. By stealing the knowledge they needed to build a plant, the Koreans avoided paying license fees for the technology, and in this way saved the enormous expense of funding a research and development program. General Electric discovered the espionage in 1992.

*Tiny synthetic diamonds in drill's tip help it cut faster*

## COMPUTER SPYING

In 1981, the FBI caught a computer engineer, Kenji Hayashi, with secret details of IBM computer disk drive technology. His employers, Japan's Hitachi corporation, gave him more than half a million dollars, which he used to bribe IBM employees. After his arrest and trial, Hitachi had to pay IBM 60 times this sum in compensation.

# Counterespionage

IN THE PAST, bugging equipment was often simple, and wires from hidden microphones sometimes led directly to the eavesdropping spies. Today, finding bugs and wiretaps – and spies who use them – is harder. It is the job of counterespionage, or counterintelligence, agencies to track them down. However, detection of spies does not always lead to their capture – sometimes an enemy spy is more valuable if allowed to carry on as normal. Working spies can provide a counterespionage agency with useful information, especially if they do not know they are being watched. A spy's activities can reveal an enemy's intelligence requirements and give away secrets about spying techniques and equipment. These details can be used to help trap other spies. Counterintelligence services also use unmasked spies to feed false information to their enemies. Sometimes, by confronting spies with evidence of their guilt, a counterespionage agency can "turn" the spies, forcing them to work against their original masters as double agents.

**SOMEONE IS WATCHING YOU**
Counterespionage agencies use many of the same tools as the spies themselves. This 19th-century cartoon makes fun of the craze for hidden cameras among spies and counterspies alike.

**KEEPING CALLS SECRET**
Devices called scramblers are sometimes used to keep telephone calls private. A typical scrambler chops speech into short segments, then rearranges these into an apparently random order for transmission along the telephone line. The "receiving" scrambler reverses the process. The people talking both use a scrambler, and they hear each other perfectly – but a spy who taps the line hears nothing but "gray noise" (a meaningless jumble).

Scrambler attached to telephone

**SETTING THE CODE**
The caller uses a row of tiny switches to set his or her scrambler to the same prearranged code as the receiving scrambler.

**COUNTERSPY'S TOOL KIT**
When checking for bugs, the counterspy uses screwdrivers and other basic tools to undo outlets and look behind light sockets and in other likely places. A visual inspection can reveal damage left when a bug was installed. By comparing cables with a wiring diagram, a counterspy can tell whether there are any other cables linking microphones to a distant transmitter.

*Rising tone in headphones indicates presence of a bug*

*Handle is removable to aid search of cramped spaces*

*Reducing power output helps pinpoint hidden bug*

*Probe detects bugs even when they are not transmitting*

**A NEW BROOM**
This device is used by a counter-espionage agent to quickly sweep (check) a room for bugs. The probe gives off a radio signal, which energizes semiconductor devices, such as transistors or integrated circuits. This creates a tell-tale signal that the "broom" detects. Innocent electronic devices such as telephones will activate the detector, but once these are taken into account, any remaining signals probably come from a concealed bug.

255 — Strength of signal

0

12 MHz

20 MHz

Frequency

*Peaks indicate where there is a bug*

## WHICH ROOM IS BUGGED?
By displaying many scans from a tuned receiver in three-dimensional form, a room that contains a bug is revealed. The graph plots signal strength and frequency in megahertz for each room of a building.

## LOOKING AROUND CORNERS
Many offices have large spaces under the floor, above the ceiling, and within the walls. These cavities are big enough to hide sophisticated and bulky monitoring equipment. To check such hiding places, counter-surveillance staff use small mirrors and tiny lights. Flexible goosenecks on the handles allow the searcher to insert the mirror deep inside inaccessible places.

*Flexible gooseneck*

*Tiny mirror reaches in smallest holes*

*High peak indicates strong signal*

*This trace indicates the presence of a bug*

*Portable computer visually interprets information from Scanlock receiver*

Cerberus 2

File   Edit   Radio   View   Windows   Help

TEST                    Location: 61      06/08/94 18:28

18.336M

*Batteries in the handle power lamps*

*Antenna picks up broadcast signals*

## SCANLOCK DETECTOR
Detecting cheap bugs is easy: play music in the suspect room, then use a radio receiver to scan commonly used frequencies. If you hear the music on the receiver there is a bug transmitter in the room. More sophisticated bugs broadcast on unusual frequencies or scramble their signals. This Scanlock wide-coverage tuned receiver picks up these "smart" bugs by scanning all the transmission frequencies within minutes.

## BUGS ON DISPLAY
Connecting the Scanlock receiver to a portable computer displays its output in visual form. The jagged lines (trace) give a skilled operator detailed information about radio signals in the surrounding area. Higher peaks indicate stronger signals. Each trace forms a picture of radio signal activity at one particular time. If a bug then switches on, its signal will change the shape of a later trace.

*Device makes high-pitched sound if it detects a bug*

*Signal strength meter leads operator to bug*

## PINPOINTING A BUG
Once counterespionage agents are sure a room is bugged, they can use a lightweight signal-strength meter to track it down. These handheld devices require no tuning and show a stronger signal the closer they are to the source.

# Spy-catching

*Intelligence officers leave court carrying Bossard's spying equipment*

LOCATING AND IDENTIFYING SPIES is rarely easy – unless a double agent or defector betrays them. Suspicious radio signals can sometimes allow counterintelligence agents to pinpoint a hidden transmitter. By tapping telephones and secretly opening mail, a counterspy can find a few spies, and patient surveillance catches many more. Careless spies sometimes give themselves away when collecting intelligence. For example, following a suspected spy can lead to the discovery of other unknown agents. Once they are caught, they must be "neutralized." This can mean exposing them so they cannot work secretly, expelling them to their home country, or prosecuting and imprisoning them. In some countries neutralization can have a more sinister meaning – a bogus trial and a death sentence.

**BLEEPS TRACE MISSILE SECRETS**
A tip-off by a defector alerted Britain's MI5 to spy Frank Bossard (b.1912). They caught him by fixing a transmitter to the files he "borrowed" from his Air Ministry office. The transmitter's radio bleeps led MI5 officers to where the spy was copying the documents.

*Probe fits through slit at top of envelope and jaws grip the letter*

**SUSPICIOUS SPY-CATCHER**
As counterespionage chief of the CIA, James Jesus Angleton (1917–87) hunted spies for two decades. He trusted nobody and suspected every defector of being a KGB double agent. He found few moles, however, and his intense suspicion slowed the agency's work. By ordering illegal mail interceptions, he damaged his reputation and was fired in 1974.

*Winding handle rolls letter into tight coil*

*Applying invisible crayon sticks powders to a surface*

*By pulling handle, agent pulls out letter*

*The Rosenbergs are taken from court after being convicted*

**FLAPS AND SEALS**
Counterespionage agents use tools like this to open letters, read them, and replace them without tearing the envelope. This skill, known as "flaps and seals," allows them to monitor letters addressed to a spy. Letters mailed by the spy, however, are much more difficult to intercept.

**ROUGH JUSTICE**
Harsh punishment of spies has sometimes aroused strong emotions. Julius and Ethel Rosenberg were caught giving secrets to the Soviet Union. They were the first American peacetime spies to be sentenced to death, and many people begged for mercy. But the two Communist spies were condemned and were put to death in the electric chair in 1953.

## SPIES ON VIDEO
Video surveillance can catch a spy at work, but checking tapes from many cameras is time-consuming. This may change with the development of digital cameras linked to computers. Once the software has "learned" what certain spies look like, it can pick them out in a crowd and start videotapes running to track the spy's movements.

*Surveillance cameras can be used to track a suspect's movements*

*SMERSH agent's identity card*

*Ultraviolet light reveals anti-bugging seals*

## SMERSH AGENCY
The Soviet counterespionage organization Smert Shpionam (roughly translated as "death to spies") was responsible for military security and for catching spies within the country's intelligence services. The agency soon acquired the nickname "SMERSH."

## CHECKING SEALS
After a bugging sweep, counter-intelligence agents use seals to secure "clean" areas. An ultraviolet lamp is used to reveal the anti-bugging stickers to check they are not broken.

## RED-HANDED
By dusting secret files with these special powders (left), counter-intelligence agents can catch a spy who handles the material. Powder sticking to the spy's hands glows under light from sources such as the ultraviolet lantern (above right).

*Screen relays signals from satellite to track small craft off the Florida coast that may be carrying drugs*

## NEW WORK
Spy-catching no longer grabs headlines as it did in the Cold War, and former counterespionage officers now find they have other duties. The CIA, for example, has established a counter-narcotics center to coordinate the activities of the American intelligence organizations in the fight against drug trafficking.

*Powder is invisible in normal light when sprinkled on files*

# Spying without spies

T HE WORK OF REAL LIVE SPIES – or HUMINT (human intelligence) – is both costly and slow, and if a spy is discovered, it could embarrass politicians. Fortunately, there are some alternatives. Technical intelligence-gathering uses remote sensors that can do the spy's work from a distance. COMINT (communications intelligence); SIGINT (signals); ELINT (electronic); and IMINT (imagery) all provide valuable knowledge. Perhaps the most important is IMINT, which is the gathering of pictures from cameras and radar in spy aircraft and satellites. These provide amazing views of objects on the ground – some can even distinguish between civilians and soldiers. Just as satellites improve a spy's distant vision, technical intelligence below ground makes other senses keener. Seabed hydrophones track the sound of enemy submarines and, like sensitive fingertips, seismographs detect the vibrations caused by atomic tests.

**SPY PLANES WITHOUT PILOTS**
*Darkstar* is a drone, or unmanned aerial vehicle (UAV), developed in the United States. UAVs can take detailed air photographs of heavily defended enemy territory without risking a pilot's life.

**SPY SATELLITE LAUNCH**
Older spy satellites used film because the pictures produced were sharper than video. The film fell to Earth in a capsule for collection and processing. Such spy satellites are still secret. This Soviet launch carries a civilian version into orbit.

Russian KFA satellite on ground after reentry

**THE EARTH FROM SPACE**
Multi-spectral images give intelligence agencies detailed pictures of war zones and military bases, but they do not show the landscape in true colors. In this image of Sarajevo in former Yugoslavia, electronic processing has made buildings stand out in pink. With greater enlargement, pictures can record objects as small as a truck.

*Sensors behind colored windows view targets in both visible light and infrared*

*Engines power the Blackbird forward three times faster than the speed of sound*

**EYES IN THE SKIES**
American Keyhole 12 spy satellites can "see" objects as small as a grapefruit from a distance of 250 miles (400 km). No nation releases pictures of its spy satellites. However, this Earth observation satellite, which is used for map-making, is built in the same way. Radar imaging allows spy satellites to look straight through cloud cover, and infrared sensors can even pick out heat shadows left by a missile launch. Multi-spectral cameras in the satellite make it possible to distinguish between real trees and camouflage.

*Aircraft is light in weight to increase range*

*Cockpit is not pressurized: pilot breathes pure oxygen from a helmet*

**U-2 SPY PLANE**
The CIA welcomed this high-flying spy plane as a triumph when it first flew in 1955 because they believed it was more accurate and dependable, and could collect information faster than any agent on the ground. The U-2 cruised at 40,000 ft (12,200 m), but this proved not high enough when a Soviet missile shot one down in 1960. The pilot was captured (pp. 38–39).

*Explosion was equivalent to an earthquake with a magnitude of 6.2 on the Richter scale*

ground up

**TRACING THE BIG BANGS**
Seismographs make vibrations in the Earth's crust visible as a trace on paper. Geologists normally use them to monitor earthquakes, but the instruments can also register underground nuclear tests on the other side of the world. In September 1949, United States intelligence analysts got their first firm evidence that the Soviet Union had developed the atom bomb from a trace like this one.

*Trace shows activity at the Soviet Union's Kazakhstan test site in central Asia*

**TAKING A CLOSE LOOK**
This is a unique photograph taken in 1984 of a Soviet aircraft carrier under construction in a Black Sea shipyard. The picture shows the ship's hull being built in two separate sections. Computer enhancement and color have improved the quality of the picture.

*Black paint is needed to dissipate heat, because friction with the atmosphere warms the plane to 800°F (427°C )*

**BLACKBIRD WITH SHARP EYES**
The *Blackbird* reconnaissance plane was built to replace the U-2. Though designed in 1959, the two-seater still flies higher and faster than any other aircraft. It can cross the Atlantic in less than two hours, and photograph a country the size of Mexico in 13 hours. Lockheed developed the U-2, the *Blackbird*, and *Darkstar* at a top-secret plant in Nevada known as the "Skunk Works." *Blackbird*s collected intelligence for more than 20 years during the Cold War, but were mothballed (taken out of service) to save money in 1990. Five years later, the US Air Force reconditioned several of the aircraft, and once more began training crews to fly surveillance missions.

# Spying today

SPIES THRIVED DURING THE COLD WAR. While it lasted, the United States and the Soviet Union feared each other's bombs and missiles, and needed intelligence agencies to help keep the peace. When the Cold War ended in the late 1980s, many spies lost their jobs. Intelligence agencies had to adapt quickly. They looked for new uses for the spies' special skills and equipment, and some even formed alliances with scientists. For example, instead of tracking submarines, America's secret hydrophone network listened to the sound of whales. Spies found that their skills in counterespionage were just as useful in counterterrorism. Intelligence agents who had trailed Cold War traitors now followed Colombian drug barons. However, not all spies accepted the role of international law enforcer. In the chaos that followed the breakup of the Soviet Union, Russian farmers planted 100,000 fields with opium poppies. All they needed were people with the right international connections to distribute the heroin they made from the poppies. There was only one choice: they recruited some of Russia's newly out-of-work spies.

**SKY-HIGH EYE**
Satellite data helps environmentalists monitor climate change and loss of habitat because of human activity or natural disaster. Spy satellites take the sharpest pictures, but until recently these have been kept secret. Now the CIA is making its images available to the general public. They will give researchers a clearer picture of how earth has changed over the last 40 years.

**DRUGS ON THE STREET**
Intelligence agencies can collect information about the production and the smuggling of narcotics. However, the war on drugs does not end when shipments reach their destination. Kits like these (left) help agents catch drug dealers. The sprays quickly identify drugs wherever they are, avoiding the cost and delay of laboratory analysis.

**EVER-CHANGING ROLE**
However much the world changes, there will always be a role for secret agents. Russia may no longer threaten the United States, but war now endangers Eastern Europe, and CIA agents have learned to speak the local Serbo-Croatian language. U.S. Secret Service agents also have an important role to play in guarding the president.

*U.S. Secret Service man protects President Bush at an anti-drug summit*

**DRUGS SNOOPER**
The war against drugs increasingly relies on American satellites that were once used to police nuclear weapons treaties. High above Colombia, a "spy in the sky" can identify jungle landing strips, drug laboratories, and storage areas. Using information gathered by satellite pictures, Colombian soldiers swoop down on the bases with helicopters and ground troops. They seized 22 tons of cocaine in a single 1994 raid.

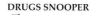

*Shoulder bag conceals a machine gun*

Fuel rod contains pellets of nuclear material

**FUELING FEAR**
Terrorists need 15.5 lb (7 kg) of plutonium from a nuclear power plant to build a bomb, and workers in Russia's crumbling nuclear industry are happy to sell it. Intelligence services across the world cooperate in tracing this stolen plutonium and uranium.

Plutonium sealed inside is highly poisonous, but radiation it emits is not a danger to bomb-makers

Lighter-fluid capsules to add to flammability

Power source (4 x 1.5-volt batteries)

Timer circuit board

Timer switch

Indicator light

Power on/off switch

**IRA BOMB**
In 1993 MI5 (Britain's counter-espionage agency) joined the police in the hunt for the IRA (Irish Republican Army) bombers. In the past the IRA has used weapons such as this fire bomb in its campaign to unite Northern Ireland (a British province) with the Irish Republic. MI5 now uses its skills to track down other activists, including some animal rights campaigners who also use fire bombs.

Compartment containing incendiary device

Fire bomb was defused before it could go off

**SHINING PATH**
Behind bars, Abimael Guzman no longer leads the Shining Path guerrilla movement that terrorized Peru for more than 20 years, killing 25,000 people. Police used spy tactics to catch him in 1992, first collecting intelligence and then staking out his apartment with agents in disguise.

**ORGANIZED CRIME**
In the United States, the FBI tracks spies and fights organized crime gangs such as the Mafia and the Chinese Triads. Counterespionage organizations, such as MI5 in Britain, have only recently joined the police in the fight.

Gamblers gather at the headquarters of New York's Hung Mon Association, which has direct links with Triad gangs

# Famous spies

THE MOST SUCCESSFUL SPIES do not become famous. As soon as their work is complete, they disappear into the shadows. Wartime spies are the exception to this. When the fighting ends, they tell their stories and sometimes earn high honors. As a reward for her spying, and for undergoing torture and imprisonment, Odette Sansom received one of Britain's most important medals, the George Cross. Not everybody believed that she deserved it. Yvonne Cormeau (pp. 32–33) complained that other SOE agents got lesser awards because "we haven't been caught." Of course all spies try to avoid capture, but if it happens, fame can quickly follow. Their captors are eager to put the spies' crimes on show. Spy trials often disappoint newspaper readers who follow them – in a real spy's life glamor is rare, and the routine boring. However, a few spies do live lives as exciting as any novel. Some actually turn into fictional characters: Ian Fleming based James Bond on the spy Dusko Popov.

Sean Connery as Bond in the film *Dr No*

**WILL THE REAL SPY STAND UP?**
Fictional James Bond (top) and real spy Dusko Popov (above with his wife) both enjoyed gambling and the company of beautiful women. Bond's creator, Ian Fleming (pp. 58–59), met Popov in 1941 when they were both secret agents.

*For her stage act, Mata Hari wore elaborate costumes and headdresses, but often danced naked as well*

*Mata Hari falsely claimed that she was the daughter of a temple dancer and that she had been dedicated to the god Shiva*

**FAILED SPY**
As Mata Hari, exotic dancer Margaretha Macleod (1876–1917) entertained German officers in France during World War I. Although she became one of the most famous names in the history of espionage, she was not very good at spying. She was recruited by the German Secret Service, but they did not entirely trust her, and she offered her services to the Allies. Germany finally betrayed her to France and on October 15, 1917, she was executed by a French firing squad.

**CODE NAME "WHITE RABBIT"**
Welsh Royal Air Force officer "Tommy" Yeo-Thomas became famous after his arrest and torture by the Gestapo, the German secret police, during World War II. He had been working for the SOE (pp. 32–33), organizing the French resistance to German troops occupying France. He was betrayed and captured outside a metro station in Paris. Tortured by the Gestapo, he was imprisoned but escaped from the death camp at Buchenwald in Germany.

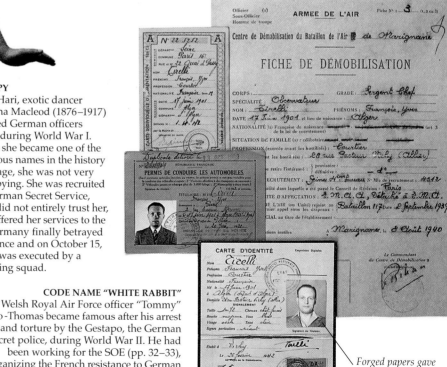

*Forged papers gave "White Rabbit" cover stories on his visits to France*

Donald Maclean (1913–83) passed atom bomb secrets to Moscow

*Odette Sansom was the first woman to win the George Cross*

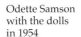
Odette Samson with the dolls in 1954

Guy Burgess (1911–63) attracted attention with his drunken violence

*Dolls entirely hand-sewn*

*Ski sticks made from card and silver foil*

Kim Philby (1912–88) warned Maclean and Burgess when to flee

### WARTIME HEROINE
During World War II, Odette Sansom (1931–95) worked as "Céline," an agent for the Allied Special Operations Executive (SOE). She helped organize resistance groups in southern France. Betrayed by a double agent in 1943, Odette was captured and taken to Fresnes Prison near Paris, where she was horribly tortured. After Fresnes, she was transferred to a prison in Germany and then to a concentration camp. Making these dolls for the nephew and niece of a German Catholic priest helped her pass the long hours of captivity. She was finally freed by the Allies in May 1945. The cruelty of her ordeal and the valor with which she faced it made her a legendary wartime spy.

Anthony Blunt (1907–83) helped the others escape to the Soviet Union

### THE CAMBRIDGE FIVE
Four of this century's most notorious spies met at Cambridge University, England. While working for Britain's Foreign Office, Guy Burgess and Donald Maclean leaked secrets to Moscow, fleeing there in 1951 when MI5 began to suspect them. When the "third man," Kim Philby (pp. 34–35), joined them in 1961, a "fourth man", Anthony Blunt, secretly admitted to spying. In return for his confession, Blunt kept his job as Surveyor of the Queen's Pictures until he retired. However, by 1979, his name had become public knowledge and, later, a "fifth man," John Cairncross, was revealed.

### SHOW-TRIAL VICTIM
Soviet military intelligence officer Oleg Penkowsky (1919–63) contacted Western intelligence agencies in 1960. He believed he could prevent war by telling the West about Soviet nuclear missiles. The secrets he provided gave the United States a real advantage in the Cold War. The KGB caught Penkowsky and he was given a show trial at which he "confessed." He was sentenced to death and reportedly executed in 1963.

# Spies in fiction

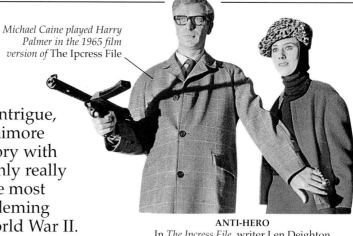

*Michael Caine played Harry Palmer in the 1965 film version of* The Ipcress File

Espionage has all the ingredients for an exciting storybook or movie: suspense, action, intrigue, and natural drama. American author James Fenimore Cooper (1789–1851) helped establish the spy story with his book *The Spy* in 1851, but spy novels have only really become popular in the last 50 years. Some of the most successful authors were themselves spies. Ian Fleming worked for British naval intelligence during World War II. John Le Carré drew on his experience of MI5 and MI6 to create a more authentic picture of the secret agent's world. Hollywood turned the books of both authors and many more into successful movies, but the books and films did not always impress real spies. Allen Dulles, once head of the CIA, wrote that "spy heroes...rarely exist in real life." This did not stop the CIA from using spy films to train agents on the finer points and pitfalls of their trade.

**ANTI-HERO**
In *The Ipcress File*, writer Len Deighton created a spy hero who shared only his nationality with James Bond. The story of the Cockney-petty-criminal-turned-reluctant-spy was Deighton's hugely successful first book.

**AUTHOR MEETS SPY**
Frederick Forsyth (left) based his book *The Odessa File* on the exploits of the German "Champagne Spy" Wolfgang Lotz (right). Lotz crippled the Egyptian missile program, helping Israel win the Six-Day War against Egypt in 1967.

*Lotz's high lifestyle earned him his nickname of "the Champagne Spy"*

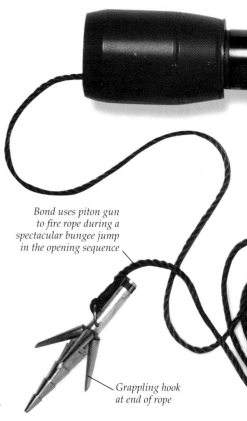

*Bond uses piton gun to fire rope during a spectacular bungee jump in the opening sequence*

*Grappling hook at end of rope*

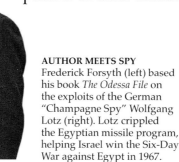

**SPY HIT LIST**
British spies may not be the world's best, but the country's espionage writers top the bestseller lists. In the 1960s, their anti-Communist message alarmed the KGB. The Soviets hit back with *The Zakhov Mission*, in which a Communist hero defeats 007. It could not compete with the success of Fleming's originals, which have been translated all over the world.

**FICTIONAL EVIL LADY**
"We are enveloped in a network of spies," cries D'Artagnan, the young hero who helps the Three Musketeers in the famous adventure story written by Alexandre Dumas (1802–1870). Milady (right) is the most deadly of the spies who are employed by Cardinal Richelieu (pp. 40–41) to try and discredit the queen of France.

**INDIAN ROPE TRICK**
High-tech gadgetry is as much the star in a Bond film as 007 himself. In the Bond books, Ian Fleming based these devices on genuine inventions supplied by people such as Charles Fraser-Smith to World War II agents (pp. 12–13).

*Buckle conceals 75-ft (27-m) long fine rope that can bear Bond's weight*

Bond's belt worn in the film *Goldeneye*

*Telescopic sights*

**TIME TOOL**
Watches play a leading role in many of the Bond films. In *Goldeneye*, a laser built into Bond's watch helps him cut his way out of difficult situations. The KGB studied James Bond films in order to develop their own spy technology.

James Bond's piton gun from the film *Goldeneye*

*Piton gun contains laser which Bond uses to cut open the roof of a Russian chemical plant*

**LICENSED TO PRINT MONEY**
When Ian Fleming (1908–64) created the character of James Bond, he was aiming to write the spy story "to end all spy stories." His 12 Bond books sold more than 18 million copies.

*In* Goldeneye, *the seventeenth James Bond film, Pierce Brosnan plays the sophisticated British spy*

*Bond primes a magnetic mine to destroy the chemical plant*

*True-to-life bugging tool kit includes lock-pick gun*

**BUGGED BATHROOM**
In the film *The Conversation*, a bugging expert (played by Gene Hackman) is drawn into a terrifying world of deception and murder. As nerve-wracking as any political spy story, the film is a rare and authentic glimpse of the work of industrial espionage agents.

# Index

# Acknowledgments

**Dorling Kindersley would like to thank:**
Audiotel International Limited (Keith Penny, Ray Summers, Julie Walker, Adrian Hickey); Eon Productions (Julie O'Reilly); the Imperial War Museum, London (Paul Cornish, John Bullen, Mike Hibbard); Intelligence Corps Museum, Ashford (Major R.W.M. Shaw, Mrs. Janet Carpenter); Leica UK Ltd (Peter Mulder); Lorraine Electronics Surveillance (David Benn, Simon Rosser); Next Retail Ltd (Shirley Brown, Hilary Santell); Joanne Poynor; Spycatcher (Mike Phillips); Whitbread plc (Nicholas Redman, Archivist)
**Design help:** Ann Cannings, Jason Gonsalves, Sailesh Patel
**Pigeon:** Rick Osman
**Pigeon parachute:** Martine Cooper
**Artwork:** John Woodcock
**Endpapers:** Iain Morris
**Index:** Marion Dent
**Picture credits**
The publisher would like to thank the following for their kind permission to reproduce the photographs:
(a = above, b = below, c = center, l = left, r = right, t = top)

AKG Photos, London / J.V. Leffdoel *Scipio Publius Cornelius* 40tl. **Ancient Art & Architecture Collection** 8tl, 8bl, 8bc. **Associated Press Ltd** 11tr, 29bl, 35t, 35br, 43c, 47bl, 52tr; Wire Photo 53cr. **Aviation Photographs International** 38tl. **Bildarchiv Preussischer Kulturbesitz** 25cl. **Bilderdienst Süddeutscher Verlag** 27cl. **Bridgeman Art Library** / Guildhall Art Gallery, Corporation of London, Sir John Gilbert, detail from *Ego Et Rex Meus* 40cl; Private Collection, I. Glasunov *Ivan the Terrible* 1989, 40bl; by courtesy of the board of Trustees of the V & A, London, Nicholas Hilliard, *Mary Queen of Scots* 28cl. **Camera Press Ltd.** 35tr, 39cl; R. Artacho 55br; S. Ferguson 42br; B. Ross 56ra. **Jean-Loup Charmet** / Bibliothèque des Arts Decoratifs, Lucien Laforge *L'Espion*, 1916, 21cl. **DC Comics, Inc.** *Spy vs. Spy* is a trademark of E.C. Publications, Inc. © 1995. All rights reserved. Used with permission 42t. **Mary Evans Picture Library** front flap tl, 29r, 40c; J. Mammen back cover tl, 14tl. **E.T. Archive** / Biblioteca Nazionale Marciana, Venice 9tr; Musée Versailles, Philippe de Champaigne,

detail from *Cardinal Richelieu* 41cr; Staatliche Glyptothek, Munich 9tl; V & A, London 11tc. **Werner Forman Archive** / Ninja Museum Ueno, detail showing Ninja making secret signs 40bl; E. Strouhal 8bl. **Ronald Grant Archive,** *Stakeout* 1987, Touchstone 16bl, *Doctor No,* 1962, UA / Eon 56tr, *The Ipcress File* 1965, Rank / Steven Lowndes 58tr, *The Three Musketeers* 1948, MGM 58br, *The Conversation* 1974, Paramount / Francis Ford Coppola 59bl. **Keith Hamshere** front cover bcl, 4cb, 9br, 59tr, 59cr, 59bl, 58-59. **Michael Holford** / Musée de Bayeux 8-9; V & A, London 10-11. **Hulton Deutsch Collection** 10cr, 38c, 41c, 41bl, 56l, 57tc, 57br, 57l. **Imperial War Museum, London** 23bc, 29tl, 36tr, 56br; Fougasse *Careless Talk Costs Lives* 10tr. **Lockheed** 52-53. **Lockheed Martin Skunk Works** 53t. **Magnum Photos Ltd** / E. Erwitt 43c; S. Meiselas 54bl; E. Reed 19cr; A. Webb 51br; Zachmann 55bl. **The Mansell Collection** 10tl. **H. Keith Melton** front cover br and bcr, back cover rcb, 13tc, 28tl, 28cr, 28tr, 28br, 30br, 37tl, 37b, 42bl, 43br, 45tl, 51cl; Jerry Richards of the FBI Laboratory, Washington, D.C. 10cl, 10c; Jack Ingram, Curator of the National Cryptologic Museum, Maryland 16cl, 16c, 27tr. **Mirror Syndication International** 27b, 50tr; Aldus Archive 24tl; Aldus Archive / Science

Museum / Eileen Tweedy front cover cr, 24cl; Rijksinstituut voor Oorlogsdocumentatie 9c; National Archives, USA 26c; Public Record Office 25tl, 41tl; © US Army 27tl. **National Cryptologic Museum, Maryland** 26bl. **National Portrait Gallery, London** / John De Critz, the Elder *Sir Francis Walsingham* 41tr. **Peter Newark's American Pictures** 30tl, 30bc, 31bl. **Popperfoto** 23tl, 31tr, 31br, 35bl, 41br, 58cl; Reuter / S. Jaffe 34br; Reuter / W. McNamee 34c. **Press Association** 36bcl. **Range** / Bettmann / UPI 22bl, 50c, 54br; Bettmann / UPI / Sam Schulman 50bc. **Rex Features Ltd** / Action Press 38-39; Sipa-Press 39tl. **Reuters Television** front cover tl, 42cr (detail), 54tl (detail). **Science Photo Library** / NRSC Ltd 52c; R. Ressmeyer, Starlight 38bc. **Science & Society Picture Library, Science Museum, London** 26tl. **Frank Spooner Pictures** / Gamma-Liaison 11cl. **Topham-Picturepoint Ltd** back cover br, 12tl, 35cla, 35c, 34tl, 34tr; AP 45tc. **Worldmap-Priroda** 52tl, 52bl.
Every effort has been made to trace the copyright holders. Dorling Kindersley apologizes for any unintentional omissions and would be pleased, in such cases, to add an acknowledgment in future editions.